DESIGNS FOR PROGRESS

DESIGNS

FOR

PROGRESS

An Introduction to

Catholic Social Doctrine

LEON McKENZIE

ST. PAUL EDITIONS

NIHIL OBSTAT:

RT. REV. MATTHEW P. STAPLETON
Diocesan Censor

IMPRIMATUR:

† RICHARD CARDINAL CUSHING
Archbishop of Boston

September 1, 1967

Printed by the *Daughters of St. Paul*
50 St. Paul's Avenue, Jamaica Plain, Boston, Mass. 02130

Contents

INTRODUCTION

One of the greatest questions of our time concerns the relevancy of religion and religious teachings in every day living. There are those who believe that religion has lost its relevancy and is hopelessly bound up in the needs of past ages, and in a rigid legalism of a mere superficial structure.

Society today has focused its attention on social crisis especially the crisis of racism and devastating poverty. Many question the relevancy of the Church to today's problems, to world poverty, to nationalism, to world community, and to economic philosophies.

Father McKenzie demonstrates that the Church and its religious teaching is most relevant to today's needs. He is an experienced and successful classroom teacher. He has long been a champion of the social doctrines of papal encyclicals, and of the necessity to make them an essential part of social studies and religious education. The documents of Vatican II, especially the Pastoral Constitution on the Church in the Modern World, have proven that his efforts have been correct. No one can deny that the social doctrines as explained herein are relevant to any topic of modern day discussion.

Designs for Progress: Introduction to Catholic Social Doctrine is written in a manner easily understood by the "reader" or the student. It will prove a valuable aid for teachers of history, sociology and religion. Indeed, it will prove a valuable aid for every thinking Christian.

REV. CHARLES W. REGAN
Superintendent of Schools
Diocese of Wichita

The Church and Society

THE PROPHETS of the Old Testament have become identified in the popular imagination as peculiar individuals who peered into the future and beheld dim visions of the coming of the Savior. It is true that prophets spoke about the advent of Christ. And it is also true that they had much to say about the future. But this isn't the whole story about the prophets.

These spokesmen for God in human history often recalled the past mercies of God to the chosen people. They urged the people to respond more lovingly to God because God first loved them and rescued them from slavery. Even more importantly, the prophets addressed themselves to the crucial social problems of their day. They boldly called attention to the plight of the poor people and pointed the finger of accusation at the high and the mighty who oppressed the poor.

The words of the fiery Amos to the women of Samaria probably did not win him any friends. Here is what he said to them: "...you cows of Basan, you who oppress the weak and abuse the needy; who say to your lords, 'Bring drink for us!' The Lord God has sworn by his holiness: Truly the days are coming upon you when they shall drag you away with hooks...." (Amos 4:1-3)

Undoubtedly Amos angered the people he condemned for defrauding the poor, "...because you have trampled upon the weak and exacted of them levies of grain, though you have built houses of hewn stone, you shall not live in them." (Amos 5:11)

The prophet Michea also turned his attention to the social evils of his day. "Woe to those who plan iniquity, and work out evil on their couches; in the morning light they accomplish it when it lies within their power. They covet fields, and seize them; houses, and they take them; they cheat an owner of his house, a man of his inheritance. Therefore says the Lord: Behold, I am planning against this race an evil from which you shall not withdraw your necks; nor shall you walk with head high, for it will be a time of evil." (Mi. 2:1-3)

Evidently Michea was confronted by critics when he preached about social evils. "'Preach not,' they preach, 'let them not preach of these things.'" (Mi. 2:6) But Michea notes with much wisdom that even if he did not preach social justice, the shame and guilt of evil men would not diminish.

The great prophet Isaia, a diplomat and adviser to King Achaz, decried the corruption of his period of history and warned against political alliances that would lead the people away from the true God. Isaia's powerful prophecies and dramatic condemnations of political and social evils eventually brought him much grief. But at least he had the satisfaction of knowing that he had delivered the messages God wanted him to deliver.

Many more examples could be given to show that the prophets were commentators on the social scene. It is sufficient for us to note, however, that God's spokesmen in the Old Testament times were concerned about the realities of the concrete order and the social situations in which men found themselves. The prophets were undoubtedly criticized for "meddling" in things that supposedly didn't concern them. We can imagine what a critic of the prophets would have said when prophetic utterances, arrow-like, found their target in a deceitful heart: "Why don't you prophets talk about heaven and God and keep your noses out of the marketplace? What business is it of yours if people are cheated? You have no right to talk about economics or business practices. You have no right to involve yourselves in political arguments."

When Christ established His Church He also established men who would speak for Him. He established a line of New Testament "prophets" to pronounce the wisdom of God in the hearing of men. We know these "prophets" familiarly as the Popes, the vicars of Christ on earth. It is through the instrumentality of the successors of St. Peter that Christ continues the work of the Old Testament prophets, insofar as social problems are concerned. God directs His people and offers reli-

gious guidance by means of His chosen spokesmen who wear the fisherman's ring. This religious
guidance given by the Holy Fathers concerns itself not only with heaven, but with the social
circumstances of the times and the daily demands
of justice and truth.

The sovereign pontiffs know very well that
religious guidance which does not go beyond a
few pious words about heaven is not authentic
religious guidance. If religious teaching is limited to sound advice about the world beyond, if
this teaching is restricted to pious platitudes, it
becomes irrelevant. It is simply "not with it."

When Pope Leo XIII wrote his great encyclical *Rerum Novarum* (On Capital and Labor) in
1891, some people argued that the Holy Father
was not competent to speak about the conditions
of the laboring man and the rights and obligations
of employers. At the beginning of *Rerum Novarum*
the Holy Father stressed that it was the "responsibility of the apostolic office" which urged him to
write about the principles of justice and truth that
should be applied to the problems faced by capital and labor. Critics argued that the responsibility of his office should urge the Pope to remain
silent about these matters.

In his encyclical *Mater et Magistra* (Christianity and Social Progress), Pope John XXIII
recalled that *Rerum Novarum*, while receiving
wide acclaim, was greeted also with "a not unex-
pected measure of opposition from some quarters."
Not realizing that the principles of justice taught
by Christ are valid for all times and must be applied to current problems, critics of Pope Leo XIII

wanted him to restrict his remarks to vague and impractical statements about the social order.

Indeed, other critics opposed even vague and impractical statements about the social problems of the day on the part of the Pope. They offered the opinion that the sovereign pontiff should "stick to religion" and not get involved in the workings of the city of man. In other words, the opponents and critics of Pope Leo XIII would have been satisfied only if the Holy Father restricted his comments to words about angels and incense, church music and candles. These critics wished to imprison Christian teachings about justice within the walls of the parish church. They wished to reduce Christian social teachings to gleaming and ineffective generalities.

Pope John ably defended the right of the sovereign pontiffs to address themselves to the social problems of the contemporary world in his remarkable encyclical *Mater et Magistra,* "...though Holy Church has the special task of sanctifying souls and making them partake of supernatural goods, she is also solicitous for the needs of men's daily life, not merely those having to do with bodily nourishment and the material side of life, but those also that concern prosperity and culture in all its many aspects and historical stages." (Paragraph 3)

The encyclical clearly indicates that since Christ was concerned about the earthly needs of men as well as their needs pertaining to eternal salvation, it is the duty of the Church to follow Our Lord's example.

"In this activity the Church is carrying out the command of her Founder, Christ, who refers primarily to man's eternal salvation when He says: *I am the way, and the truth and the life*, and *I am the light of the world*. But when, gazing about at the hungry crowd, He sighs, as it were, and cries out: *I have compassion on this multitude*, he makes plain His concern also for the earthly needs of men. The divine Redeemer offers proof of this concern not only by His words but also in the deeds of His life, as when to alleviate the hunger of a crowd He more than once miraculously multiplies bread." (Paragraph 4)

The voices of the bishops of the world, articulated in the pastoral constitution of Vatican II *The Church in the Modern World*, direct God's people to take a more active part in shaping society according to correct principles.

"Let everyone consider it his sacred obligation to esteem and observe social necessities as belonging to the primary duties of modern man. For the more unified the world becomes, the more plainly do the offices of men extend beyond particular groups and spread by degrees to the whole world. But this development cannot occur unless individual men and their associations cultivate in themselves the moral and social virtues, and promote them in society; thus, with the needed help of divine grace men who are truly new and artisans of a new humanity can be forthcoming." (Paragraph 30)

The Fathers of the Council spoke often about social complexities and problems only because they felt it their duty to do so, a duty entrusted to them by Christ.

The Church does not wish to intrude in the workings of the city of man where she does not belong. Neither the Popes nor the Fathers of Vatican II desire to dictate to people how they should run their businesses, how to vote or what crops to plant. The Church does not wish to deprive men of their freedom to determine their economic, social or political destinies. But the Church does insist that whatever courses men take in the economic, social or political fields must meet the requirements of justice and truth. Men should not neglect God's commandments with the unreasonable excuse that His commandments interfere with their freedoms. Men are never to be considered independent of the norms of justice in their dealings with other men, whatever those dealings might be.

Economic, social or political systems have no right to function independent of the rules for ethical behavior. And any system that threatens the dignity and well-being of men, any system that opposes itself to truth and justice, must be denounced vigorously by the Holy Fathers, by the bishops and priests and by all members of God's family.

Man has been defined by some as an economic animal; by others as a social animal; by still others as a political animal. Each of these definitions is partially correct. But we must never forget that man is, or should be, primarily a religious animal. If his religious principles do not touch upon his economic, social and political judgments, then his religious principles are valueless. Religion becomes little more than a quaint custom if it is not put into practice in a person's everyday life. It is not enough for Christians to trot out the banner of the cross on Sunday. They must *live* their Christian principles each day of the week, in every circumstance of life.

The Son of God became incarnate in human history to reveal the will of His heavenly Father. He came also to change the course of human events. He wished to direct the course of human events to a fitting conclusion. Thus it is that the followers of Christ work today for the realization of God's will "on earth as it is in heaven." Every follower of Christ is challenged to transform the world after the pattern enunciated by Christ in His sermon on the mount. And to change the world it is necessary to transform the economic, social and political structures of the world.

Social action, of course, is not enough. *Knowledge* must precede action if action is to be more than mere nervous activity. The Holy Fathers have spoken to us and have outlined Christian approaches to social problems. They have fulfilled their vocation as "prophets" of the New Testament. It is now up to us to fulfill our vocations as ambassadors of Christ to the twentieth century. If we fail in this we are something less than authentic Christians and we "mutilate" Christianity. The great churchman Leon Cardinal Suenens of Belgium makes this very clear:

"One of the chief merits of our age has been to recall that Christ is not alone the life of the soul, but the life of the whole man, and that nothing is independent of His action, be it family or professional life, civic or economic activities, national or international interests, the laws of marriage or of education, men's leisure hours, the press, the cinema, the radio, television or the application of nuclear energy. To restrict Christianity to a few pious exercises, however important, is to mutilate it." (*The Gospel to Every Creature,* Newman Press.)

We know that the world cannot be Christianized if the social order remains untouched by the consecrating hand of Christ. Christian principles, as embodied in the papal encyclicals, must pervade all levels of society. The leaven of Christian justice must permeate the entire dough. This permeation will take place only if we become aware of our role in solving these problems; only if our social action is based on a thorough knowledge of Christian principles and Christian approaches to social problems.

The study of papal encyclicals is not easy. There are many more interesting things to do than to study an encyclical. But the question we must answer is this: Are there more *important* things? The degree of our personal maturity will be measured by the answer we give to this question.

PROJECTS:
1. Find examples in the Old Testament of the prophets' concern for social justice.
2. Find examples in the New Testament of Christ's concern for the earthly needs of men.
3. How is *Rerum Novarum* translated? *Quadragesimo Anno? Mater et Magistra?* How do encyclicals get their official names?
4. Give an example of a present-day social evil and show how it contradicts the message of the gospel.
5. Prepare a bulletin board display illustrating how students can go about correcting abuses in society.

DISCUSSION QUESTIONS:

1. Why are some people critical of the Holy Fathers when they speak out about social problems?
2. What measures can the student take to become a more effective instrument for the Christianization of society?
3. Do any of the clubs or organizations in your school or parish engage in Christian social study or Christian social action? Should they?
4. Explain the following statement: "If Catholics do not follow the social encyclicals in their lives, the Church begins to appear irrelevant to modern man."
5. If you have done nothing to better the social order in the last week, is it a matter for confession? Explain your answer.

The Church
and Capitalism

BEFORE WE EXAMINE some of the teachings of the Church regarding capitalism it will be necessary to turn our attention to another word — economics. Since capitalism is a system of economics, it would be foolish to begin talking about capitalism if we had no idea of the nature of economics.

"Economics" comes from a Greek word *oikonomos*. This word can be translated roughly as "household." George Soule, an economist, tells us that the housekeeper "has to see that there is enough food, clothing, and shelter, that the house is kept in order, that the necessary duties are performed by appropriate members of the household, and that their products are distributed according to necessity or custom." (*Ideas of the Great Economists*, New American Library) The economist, therefore, can be likened to a householder who attempts to keep things running smoothly and in good order.

As everyone knows, there are many different ways or systems of keeping house. Likewise are there many different approaches to the ordering of national and international monetary policies, credit terms, wage standards and so forth. History records that many people have devised procedures or systems of putting into order the accumulation and distribution of worldly goods.

Plato, Aristotle, St. Thomas Aquinas, Adam Smith, David Ricardo, Karl Marx, Thorstein Veblen and John Maynard Keynes are but a few of the many people who have devoted much thought to the complexities of economics. Some of these men, and many others too, have developed entire systems of economics and have written books describing these systems. (George Soule's book *Ideas of the Great Economists* is an excellent introduction to the history of economic thought.)

But now back to capitalism, one of the systems of keeping financial houses in order. Capitalism is a system which is:

1) based on the right of private property
2) by which material gains are accumulated
3) through investment and
4) the profit motive.

This is merely a general description of the capitalist system of economics. To be complete our description would have to take into consideration such things as prices, market values, tariffs, etc. The description given here, however, is sufficient for a basic understanding of capitalism.

In its earlier form capitalism was identified with what was called the doctrine of *laissez faire*.

Some economists thought that the State should have nothing to do with the business enterprises of its citizens. It was thought that there was some sort of a "natural law" which governed economic matters and that interference in any way on the part of the State or civil laws would disrupt the economic balance and bring disaster.

Laissez faire could be translated non-literally as "hands off." *Laissez faire* economists argued that the capitalist—the one who invested money and/or owned a business—should be allowed *absolute* freedom in determining how he used his money and what business policies he should follow. It was maintained that the capitalist should possess this freedom because he possessed an absolute right to his wealth.

It was also thought that the profit motive, the owner's desire for increased gains through investment, would automatically insure the right use of wealth and would automatically bring about the growth of business. More jobs and better wages for employees meant more buyers and larger markets. More buyers and larger markets meant a continued growth of business. A continued growth of business meant more jobs and better wages. And as the circle swung around the capitalist would reap profits from his investments. The theory sounds very good. But *laissez faire* economists failed to take into account man's fallen nature and his inclinations to greed.

In the last century there was a rapid development in the means of production. Factories were built and people flocked to the cities to gain employment. This phenomenon is known as the industrial revolution. The industrial revolution produced much wealth and affluence, but it also produced much misery. Something went wrong with the "natural law" that was supposed to regulate economic progress. Economic liberalism and unrestricted free enterprise had failed to produce a well-ordered society. By and large the workingman found it more and more difficult to survive economically and to preserve his human dignity.

It was not unusual at the height of the industrial revolution to find small children laboring 60 hours a week in factories. And it was commonplace to see men working longer than 60 hours a week in sub-human conditions and for salaries that were unjust. Pope John wrote:

"While enormous riches accumulated in the hands of a few, workingmen in vast numbers found themselves contending daily with grinding economic hardships. Wages were insufficient or even, in some instances, at a starvation level; working conditions imposed on wage earners in the lower brackets were oppressive and destructive of physical health, moral behavior and religious faith. Especially inhuman were the working conditions to which children and women were often subjected. The specter of involuntary unemployment was ever present to the worker's mind. Family life stood exposed to a process of gradual disintegration." (*Mater et Magistra*, Paragraph 13)

The former plight of the coal miners in our own country exemplifies the sorry state of affairs that visited the workingmen. Their condition has been dramatized in popular song. In the lyrics of

"Sixteen Tons" we learn of a man who mined coal all day and yet was unable to purchase back his "soul" from the company store. Huge coal companies would pay men mere pittances for their hard work, but would provide easy credit for the miners at a store owned by the coal companies. The result was that in many places coal miners were reduced to an economic slavery, working out their lives attempting to pay their bills.

Coal companies are not singled out because we have any particular bones to pick with them. The condition of the laboring man was about the same in practically all branches of industry. The cotton mills of the New England states, for example, furnish clear evidence of the intolerable conditions under which the working man and his family attempted to eke out a miserable existence.

The encyclical *Rerum Novarum* was written to assist the working man in attaining a larger share of human dignity through his labors. Pope Leo XIII taught that the remuneration for labor "must be enough to support the wage earner in reasonable and frugal comfort." (Paragraph 45) The Holy Father also stressed that civil authority and law should protect the workingman from the rapacious greed of those who would exploit him. "Justice demands that the interests of the working classes should be carefully watched over by the administration, so that they who contribute so largely to the advantage of the community may themselves share in the benefits which they create—that being housed, clothed, and bodily fit, they may find their life less hard and more endurable." (Paragraph 34) Pope Leo made it clear that the State should not become supreme nor absorb the individual or his family. But the State must protect the general welfare of the populace through due process of law.

Laissez faire capitalism failed because investors and owners desired too much of a return for their investments. They did not realize that although man has a right to private property, he also has an obligation to use his property and wealth responsibly. Man's right to wealth is always relative to the common good or general welfare of society. For many capitalists the profit motive became the sole standard of human activity. This brought low wages and poor working conditions for the laborers.

The principles of *Rerum Novarum* were reaffirmed in the encyclical *Quadragesimo Anno* (On Reconstructing the Social Order) in 1931 by Pope Pius XI.

"Every effort must be made that the fathers of families receive a wage large enough to meet ordinary family needs adequately." (Paragraph 71)

"Social justice cannot be said to have been satisfied as long as workingmen are denied a salary that will enable them to secure proper sustenance for themselves and for their families; as long as they are denied the opportunity of acquiring a modest fortune and forestalling the plague of universal pauperism; as long as they cannot make suitable provision through public or private insurance for old age, for periods of illness or unemployment." (Paragraph 52)

The Holy Fathers likewise have asserted the rights of workingmen to join unions (associations) for collective bargaining. This teaching was strengthened in our own times by Pope John:

"Pope Leo also defended the worker's natural right to enter into association with his fellows. Such association may consist either of workers alone or of workers and employers, and should be structured in a way best calculated to safeguard the workers' legitimate professional interests. And it is the natural right of the workers to work without hindrance, freely, and on their own initiative within these associations for the achievement of these ends." (*Mater et Magistra*, Paragraph 22)

It must be noted that the Holy Fathers did not deny the right of private ownership and investment as did the radical socialists and communists. We shall learn more about this in the following chapter. For now it is sufficient to point out that Pope Leo XIII forcefully attacked the error of those who denied the right to private property. He wrote: "...they assail the right of property sanctioned by the natural law; and by a scheme of horrible wickedness, while they seem desirous of caring for the needs and satisfying the desires of all men, they strive to seize and hold in common whatever has been acquired, by title of lawful inheritance, or by labor of brain and hands, or by thrift in one's mode of life." (*Quod Apostolici Muneris*, "On Socialism," Paragraph 2)

In *Mater et Magistra* Pope John quotes in defense of the right of private ownership delivered in a radio speech of Pope Pius XII on September 1, 1944:

"In defending the principle of private property the Church is striving after an important ethico-social goal. She does not intend solely and merely to uphold the present state of affairs as if it were an expression of the Divine Will or to protect on principle the rich and plutocrats against the poor and indigent.... The Church rather aims at seeing to it that the institution of private property is such as it should be according to the plan of Divine Wisdom and the dispositions of nature." (Paragraph 111)

Pope John goes on to indicate the social function of private ownership. (Paragraphs 119, 120, 121) The "haves" are obliged to contribute to the "have-nots" in such a way that the total society benefits.

There is nothing intrinsically wrong with the profit motive either. In fact, the profit motive is the only practical incentive to work, as the Russian communists are discovering today. But when the profit motive for material wealth becomes the all-surpassing norm, when it is regulated neither by the laws of God nor the laws of man, then it becomes a god. Unrestricted capitalism becomes a form of materialism as vicious as communism.

Unfortunately, in our own 20th century America we sometimes hear the glories of *laissez faire* capitalism celebrated. We are told that free enterprise and the right to private property is the "American Way." We are told that what a man does with his wealth is nobody else's business; that private ownership does not bring with it an obligation to use this wealth for the general welfare of society.

There are some people today, for example, who are violently anti-communist not because communism represents a threat to justice and truth, but because communism represents a threat to *laissez faire* capitalism. By some strange logic God is recruited on the same side as *laissez faire* capitalists. We are given to believe that God frowns on communism because He is the Supreme Capitalist.

To sum up: The Church states that capitalism is a permissible economic system if it is regulated by law. The profit motive is not wrong as long as it is not the sole motive of human actions. Free enterprise is to be encouraged if this is also a responsible free enterprise. Man has a natural right to own property and to invest capital, but his right is always relative to the general welfare of society. It is not an absolute right.

These are important principles to remember and to put into action. So important are they that the progress of humanity and the ordering of the social structure depend upon them. Happily many modern capitalists are recognizing the validity of these principles. As a result we can see a capitalism in action that is truly responsible and conscious of its social obligations. It is this sort of capitalism that can assist modern man in building a better future.

PROJECTS:
1. Refer to the encyclopedia for articles concerning the economic ideas of: Plato, St. Thomas Aquinas, Adam Smith, Karl Marx, Thorstein Veblen and John Maynard Keynes. Each member of the class could research these economists and represent one of them in a panel discussion.
2. Refer to encyclopedias and dictionaries for more complete definitions of capitalism.

3. Go to the library and try to discover how the ideas of Charles Darwin influenced ideas in economics.
4. Write to a Labor Union and ask for materials that explain the aims and goals of the Union movement in this country.
5. Invite a business man to your class to explain his ideas on capitalism.

DISCUSSION QUESTIONS:

1. How would you explain the social function of wealth to a man who would say, "What is mine is mine and I intend to spend my money only as *I* please"?
2. Discuss the morality of graduated income taxes. (Taking more taxes from the rich than from the poor.)
3. Explain the following statement: "Every economic system, to be valid and true, must take man as he really is; that is, as a person with a fallen human nature."
4. How can the government regulate capitalism without interfering in personal freedoms?
5. Give examples of excessive stress on the profit motive in our society — the "what's in it for me" attitude.

The Church
and Communism

IN PREPARING AN encyclical the sovereign pontiffs always formulate their judgments in the light of the teachings of Our Lord. Futhermore, the Holy Fathers rely heavily on the advice and suggestions of people who are "in the know" about social complexities. An encyclical is not a spur of the moment document; it is not written on impulse. Every Pope has available scores of priests and laymen who specialize in different social questions and who assist in the composition of each encyclical.

The brilliant insights and sagacious plans embodied in papal encyclicals are sometimes the result of years of study and analysis by hundreds of men who weigh each sentence of the encyclical with utmost care. The Holy Father examines their work, adapts their ideas to his own aims and then promulgates the encyclical.

We have taken pains to point out how an encyclical is composed to contrast encyclicals with the social commentaries produced by so-called revolutionaries. We shall examine some of the ideas of these revolutionaries later in this chapter.

The reaction of the Holy Fathers to *laissez faire* capitalism and to the crucible of human suffering constructed by the industrial revolution was a reaction that was at once realistic and just. Papal reaction, based on the teachings of Christ, was not "reactionary" in the sense of being extreme. The moderate and carefully balanced approach of the encyclicals to social problems recognized human limitations and human frailty. This approach also recognized that the remedies for a healthy social order would necessarily have to be founded on the virtue of justice. The encyclicals sided neither with the rich nor the poor, but with justice — the virtue which enables us to give to each man what is his due.

The responses of some people in the last century to the social situation were reckless and extreme. Many social documents and commentaries, responses to abused human dignity, were written in the heat of revolutionary passion and emotion. Christian principles were cast aside. Indeed, the fervor of the revolutionary sometimes inclined him to neglect even the dictates of right reason.

This is not to say that everything written by social revolutionaries was untrue. We merely wish to note that social revolutionaries produced systems of economic and social reform under circumstances which did not contribute to clarity of vision or realistic and just judgments.

A case in point would be the example of the social reformers we know as socialists.

Some of the early socialists, even prior to the industrial revolution, were so moved by the poverty of the masses that they militantly preached the theft of all private property by the State, the abolishment of all inheritance rights and the distribution of all wealth to the masses by the government. One social reformer, Francois Babeuf, went so far as to teach that only those who did useful work should have rights; that men and women, to be completely equal, must dress alike; that children should be taken from their parents to be indoctrinated by the State. Other socialists taught similarly extreme ideas.

Now when we talk about socialism we must understand exactly what is meant by the word. In its original form socialism was a doctrine which denied individual liberty and enthroned the State as supreme. Pure socialism meant that man was a creature of the State and that no institution, not even the Church, possessed any rights not granted and bestowed by the State. No wonder Pope Leo XIII so roundly condemned this pernicious teaching.

"At the very beginning of Our pontificate, as the nature of Our apostolic office demanded, we hastened to point out in an encyclical letter addressed to you, venerable brethren, the deadly plague that is creeping into the very fibers of society and leading it on to the verge of destruction. ...We speak of that sect of men who, under vari-

ous and almost barbarous names, are called socialists, communists or nihilists..." (*Quod
Apostolici Muneris*, Paragraph 1)

"The nihilists" mentioned by Pope Leo were
social revolutionaries who went to the extreme
of teaching that government was wrong because
the civil authority alledgedly protected only
those who were wealthy. These radicals wished
to do away with all forms of government and
reduce society to a state of anarchy—a sort of
jungle existence where the mob ruled and where
the impoverished took anything they needed
from the wealthy.

Today the term "socialism" is an ambiguous
term. It can be understood in many senses. In
some countries there are even political parties
designated as Christian Socialist parties to indicate their interest in allowing the State or government to take a greater role in social welfare. Some
modern Christian socialists do not believe that
the State is supreme and the source of all rights,
but that the State alone is competent to face up
to the complexities involved in promoting the
common good by means of social legislation and
programs to help the needy.

Some socialists today are as far removed from
19th century socialists as the modern capitalist
is removed from his 19th century counterpart.
Certainly there are extreme capitalists in our
midst today and there are extreme socialists, but
we must be careful not to think in terms of blan-
ket designations or labels. Labels have a way of
remaining the same while the reality which wears
the label changes. A modern Christian socialist,

for example, would praise Pope John for some of his directives in *Mater et Magistra*.

"Where the State fails to act in economic affairs when it should, or acts defectively, incurable civil disorders are seen to follow. Likewise, unscrupulous men of power—whose breed, alas grows in every age and place like cockle among the wheat—take advantage of the weak for their own wicked gain." (Paragraph 58)

If we wish to find the true socialist today, we would have to look in the direction of Russia and China. These regimes are close descendants of original socialist doctrines and systems. They are built, in fact, upon the foundation laid by Karl Marx.

Many good books are available in which the social, political and philosophical ideas of Karl Marx are presented with great skill. Nor are we lacking in books which describe the fallacies and gross errors of Marxism. It will be sufficient here, therefore, to present only a brief survey of the Marxist brand of socialism and to manifest papal teachings in regard to Marxism.

Marxism is a type of socialism which promises to lead to the establishment of communism—a utopia of material splendor where all the earthly needs of men will be satisfied.

Karl Marx was born in 1818 and died in 1883. Like the Holy Fathers, Marx was saddened by the tragedies that befell the workingmen during the industrial revolution. He was especially angered at the abuse human dignity received at the hands of *laissez faire* capitalists. For this reason Marx spent his whole life trying to destroy the capitalist system of economics.

Unlike the Holy Fathers, Marx was guided neither by Christian principles nor the principles of the natural law regarding justice and equity. The extreme response of Marx to abused human dignity led him on to develop a system which, while attempting to restore dignity to the workingman, abused human dignity even more than the approaches of *laissez faire* capitalism.

In 1848, together with Frederich Engels, Marx composed a short dramatic document called "The Communist Manifesto." Marx spent the remainder of his life expanding the ideas contained in the "Manifesto" and wrote many articles and books defending his notions.

Marx had no room for God in his plans. He believed that the laws of history decreed a class struggle between the rich and poor which would ultimately lead to the establishment of the communist state. Marx had little to say about how a socialistic society should be run. In other words, he was short on political ideas. This vacuum in Marx's thought was filled in by Lenin and the Russian revolutionaries who opted in favor of a totalitarian system of dictatorship.

The ringing words of "The Communist Manifesto," particularly the opening words — "A specter is haunting Europe: the specter of communism" — and the concluding words — "Workers have nothing to lose but their chains. They have a world to win. Workers of the world, unite!" — were grist for the mills of many assorted social revolutionaries who had little more going for them besides strong lungs, frantic fervor and hatred of the rich.

In the early part of this century one of these social revolutionaries, N. Lenin, was instrumental in structuring Russian society along the lines mapped out by Marx. After the Bolsheviks had overthrown the Russian Czars, Lenin promoted the teachings of Marx with great success. Thus it is that the Russian and Chinese regimes today argue with each other as to which regime is authentically "Marxist-Leninist."

Marxist socialism has been repeatedly rejected by the Holy Fathers, and for various reasons. Pope Leo saw in true socialism an attempt "to subvert all revelation, and overthrow the supernatural order." He described the teachings of socialism as "a new species of impiety, unheard of even among the heathen nations" by which "states have been constituted without any count at all of God or of the order established by Him." Pope Leo goes on in *Quod Apostolici Muneris* to point out that the truths of faith are assailed by socialism as hostile to human reason, and that "the rewards and punishments of a future and eternal life having been handed over to oblivion, the ardent desire of happiness has been limited to the bounds of the present." (Paragraph 2)

Pope Pius XI rejected Marxism in his famous encyclical *Divini Redemptoris* (On Atheistic Communism).

"The Communism of today, more emphatically than similar movements in the past, conceals in itself a false messianic idea. A pseudo-ideal of justice, of equality and fraternity in labor impregnates all its doctrines and activity with a deceptive mysticism, which communicates a zealous and contagious enthusiasm to the multitudes entrapped by delusive promises." (Paragraph 8)

"Communism...strips man of his liberty, which is the principle of his life as a rational being, robs the human person of all his dignity and removes all the moral restraints that check the eruptions of blind impulse. There is no recognition of any right of the individual in his relations to the collectivity; no natural right is accorded to the human person, who becomes a mere cogwheel in the Communist system." (Paragraph 10)

The late Father Teilhard de Chardin, following the same lines of thought of the sovereign pontiffs, truly adjudged the collective paradise of Karl Marx to be little more than "the ant-hill instead of brotherhood."

To be sure the State must take a hand in assisting the citizens to build a better tomorrow. In *Mater et Magistra* Pope John re-stated that economic growth and progress is basically due to the initiative of private citizens, but that circumstances arise in which public authorities "must play an active role in promoting increased productivity with a view to social progress and the welfare of all citizens." (Paragraph 52) Pope John recalled one of the most important principles of Catholic social philosophy, the principle of subsidiarity. This principle was first enunciated by Pius XI and is re-emphasized in *Mater et Magistra*: "Just as it is wrong to withdraw from the individual and commit to the community at large what private enterprise and endeavor can accomplish, so it is likewise unjust and a gravely harmful disturbance of right order to turn over to a greater society of higher rank functions and services which can be performed by lesser bodies on a lower plane. For a social undertaking of any sort, by its very nature, ought to aid the members of the body social, but never destroy and absorb them." (Paragraph 53)

In other words, the principle of subsidiarity demands that social reforms which can be competently handled by private persons or organizations should not become the concern of the community at large or the State. This principle of subsidiarity is perhaps the most realistic social principle ever designed. It admits the right to private property and the right of individuals to do those things they *can* do; it admits the right, and obligation, of the State to execute reforms that are beyond the ability of individuals to achieve.

Not to follow the principle of subsidiarity is to fall into the error of individualism and *laissez faire*, or the error of Marxism which looks to the State as supreme. The principle of subsidiarity enables us to make our way between the devil and the deep blue sea without falling victim to either.

In the last chapter on "The Church and Capitalism" and in this chapter we can see that there are two forms of materialism in the modern world which threaten the total well-being of man: The materialism of unrestrained capitalism and the materialism of Marxism or communism. Both of these materialistic views of life are based on the assumption that man is merely a material being who had better get whatever he can in this life because there is no reward or punishment after the present earthly existence. Both forms of materialism contradict the scriptural truth that men do not live by bread alone but by every word that proceeds from the mouth of God.

The welfare of humanity demands that Christians everywhere rise up to win the world for justice and truth. It is only by acting upon Christian social principles that this two-headed dragon of materialism will be slain. When this occurs man will be able to take sure steps down the road that leads to a better world.

PROJECTS:

1. Find passages in *Rerum Novarum, Quadragesimo Anno* and *Mater et Magistra* that point out the errors of communism.
2. Stage a debate between a *laissez faire* capitalist and a communist. Members of the class should take the parts of the debaters.
3. Conduct a panel discussion concerning some social welfare programs of the government. Apply the principle of subsidiarity to these programs.
4. Write an essay on the theme: "Man Does Not Live by Bread Alone."
5. Write a brief biography of Karl Marx, Frederich Engels or N. Lenin.

DISCUSSION QUESTIONS:

1. How can a Christian be a "socialist"? Can a Christian be a *true* socialist?
2. What are some practical ways to work for the victory of

justice and truth over communism?

3. If the State is not the source of human rights, where are we to find this source?

4. Should Christians communicate with communists today for purposes of dialogue and discussion?

NOTE: A very interesting and amusing book to be read in conjunction with this chapter is *Animal Farm* by George Orwell.

The Church
and Human Rights

ASK ANYONE "What is man?" and you will be able to deduce his entire philosophy of life from his answer. What we think of man and how we value individual persons influences our judgments about society. Society, after all, is composed of men. Our appreciation of man's ultimate destiny affects profoundly the way we look at our fellow human beings; it affects profoundly the way we look at ourselves.

The French encyclopedist who defined man as "a dirty insect who wallows on a vast blob of mud" will look at human beings differently than would Emerson, who described man as a "divinity in disguise." Certainly the treatment a person would receive at the hands of the encyclopedist would be different from the treatment and respect he would receive from Emerson.

Before we consider the matter of human rights, before we consider what those rights are and where they come from, we must first state our position regarding the nature and destiny of man.

There are some men today who believe that man is merely a clever animal, removed from other animals only by the degree of his cleverness. For these people man is merely a biological specimen whose final destiny is to be mingled with the dust after providing a sumptuous meal for worms. Death, for some men, signifies not a return to God but merely a return to the bosom of mother earth.

Atheistic communists regard man as a tool of the State. Only the "collective" man counts as far as Marxists are concerned. Only the ant-hill is important. Man possesses a dignity only insofar as he is able to contribute to the coming to be of the communist earthly paradise.

It invariably happens when men begin their philosophies of life with a rejection of God that they eventually reach a point where they reject man! Judgments about man's value and ultimate destiny are closely linked with a person's judgments about God. That is why the truest thing we can say about communism is not that it is untrue, but that it is irrelevant and even inhuman. If God, the Ultimate Norm and Source of Value, does not exist, then nothing is valuable.

What the Church thinks about man is derived from what the Church thinks about God. The Church recognizes God as the Creator who made man in His own image and likeness. The Church, therefore, recognizes the grandeur of the individual person. The Church recognizes and teaches that man possesses an invaluable dignity.

But the Church also teaches that man has inherited a fallen human nature, that every man is born into a situation of alienation from God. Man is a paradox. Or as Blaise Pascal put it: "Man is both the glory and the scandal of the universe."

The fact of man's fallen human nature does not lessen man's dignity. Man's dignity as a child of God remains because of man's destiny. If the individual person cooperates with God's graces, he is destined to participate in the joys of heaven. He is called by God in Christ to share in the family life of the Blessed Trinity. Beyond his natural dignity as an enfleshed spirit, man possesses a supernatural dignity. The very Son of God assumed to Himself the human nature in which we all share. "The Word became flesh." Every man is either a member of the mystical body of Christ, or a potential member of that mystical body. Every man, therefore, is unspeakably precious. Whatever we do in regard to our fellow human beings, whether it be giving a cup of cold water or a kind word, we do to Christ.

The Church's teaching on the nature of man and his dignity has been articulated for hundreds of years. Sacred Scripture, the Fathers of the Church and the sovereign pontiffs have always stated the Church's teachings regarding man explicitly, clearly and vigorously.

In the encyclical *Pacem in Terris*, Pope John re-stated the Church's teaching in these words: "If we look upon the dignity of the human person in the light of divinely revealed truth, we cannot help but esteem it far more highly. For men are redeemed by the blood of Jesus Christ. They are by grace the children and friends of God and heirs of eternal glory." (Paragraph 10)

Once we have admitted that man possesses a dignity and destiny that have been bestowed upon him by Almighty God, it must necessarily follow that we admit human rights. Pope Pius XII made this clear in his Christmas message of 1942. He also went on to outline briefly some of the steps that must be taken to honor the rights of men.

"The dignity of the human person requires normally as a foundation of life the right to the use of the goods of the earth. To this right corresponds the fundamental obligation to grant private ownership of property.... Positive legislation regulating private ownership may change and more or less restrict its use. But if legislation is to play its part in the pacification of the community, it must prevent the worker...from being condemned to an economic dependence and slavery which is irreconcilable with his rights as a person. Whether this slavery arises from the exploitation of private capital or from the power of the State, the result is the same."

Not only is the State or body politic forbidden to deprive man of his rights, the State must also regulate, when necessary, the economic order and the social order in such a way that the rights of men are protected.

Pope John stressed that the rights of man flow directly from his human nature as an intelligent and free agent. "Any human society, if it is to be well-ordered and productive, must lay down as a foundation this principle, namely, that every human being is a person, that his nature is endowed with intelligence and free will. By virtue of this, he has rights and duties of his own, flowing directly and simultaneously from his very nature. These rights are therefore universal, inviolable and inalienable." (*Pacem in Terris*, Paragraph 9)

Those who have read the Constitution of the United States will see how closely American ideals approach the principles outlined by Pope John. "We hold these truths to be self-evident, that all men are created equal, that they are endowed by their Creator with certain inalienable Rights, that among these are Life, Liberty and the pursuit of Happiness."

Pope John noted that human rights are universal, inviolable and inalienable, that is, *every* human being is the possessor of these natural rights, which are not to be violated or taken away from him.

But what are some of these rights specified by the Holy Father?

The sovereign pontiff listed the right to life, to bodily integrity and to the means which are necessary and suitable for the development of life. These are the most basic of human rights. The *means* for the proper development of life are food, clothing, shelter, rest, medical care and the social services. (*Pacem in Terris*, Paragraph 11) In the same paragraph of *Pacem in Terris* the Holy Father stated that man has natural rights to *secu-*

rity in case of illness, the inability to work, forced unemployment and/or old age.

But these are not all of the rights guaranteed by the natural law.

"By the natural law, every human being has the right to respect for his person, to his good reputation, to freedom in searching for truth and — within the limits laid down by the moral order and the common good—in expressing and communicating his opinions, and in pursuit of art. He has the right, finally, to be informed truthfully about public events." (Paragraph 12)

"The natural law also gives man the right to share in the benefits of culture, and therefore the right to a basic education or to technical or professional training in keeping with the stage of educational development in the country to which he belongs." (Paragraph 13)

"Every human being has the right to honor God according to the dictates of an upright conscience, and the right to profess his religion privately and publicly." (Paragraph 14)

Pope John continued his enumeration of the rights that belong to man by reason of the natural law when he listed:

1) The right to choose freely the state of life a man prefers.

2) Parents have a prior right, that is, a right that cannot be gainsaid by the State, to support and educate their children.

3) Men have a natural right to free initiative in economic enterprises. This right, of course, must always be exercised with an eye toward the common good. Men have a right to work.

4) Men have a right to private property, always recognizing the social function of private property.

5) Men have the right of assembly and association.

6) The right to freedom of movement and residence within the confines of one's own country belongs to all men. When there is a just cause, men have the right to emigrate to other countries. The Holy Father points out quite clearly that citizenship in a particular country does not take away a man's membership in the human family.

7) All men have a right to take active part in public affairs.

It would be well for everyone, especially high school students to take to heart what Pope John said about man's right to respect for his person and a good reputation. Our dealings with high school students over the years have indicated to us that they can be heartless when dealing with one another, even to the extent of denying respect to individuals because they are not members of the "in" group.

Parents should keep in mind that all men, even their children, have a right to determine freely their state in life. Parents should assist their children in determining a state in life by advising them. But parents who insist that their children enter into this or that state of life and who attempt to coerce their children are depriving them of a basic human right.

Since these human rights listed by Pope John are possessed by reason of the natural law, every other person is commanded by force of the natural law to respect these rights. Since every right enumerated by the Pope means that there is a corresponding duty to recognize that right, the list of duties is always as long as the list of rights.

If a Negro family has the right to move into a predominantly white neighborhood, or anywhere for that matter, everyone has the duty to honor this right. If the people of India have a right to the means of life, food, shelter and clothing, we have a duty to respect that right and to do all in our power to allow for the free exercise of that right.

"It is not enough, for example, to acknowledge and respect every man's right to the means of subsistence. One must also strive to insure that he actually has enough in the way of food and nourishment." (*Pacem in Terris*, Paragraph 32)

Pope John had a good reason for discussing human rights at great length in *Pacem in Terris*. He tells us that when "...the relations of human society are expressed in terms of rights and duties, men become conscious of spiritual values and understand the meaning and significance of truth, justice, charity and freedom." (Paragraph 45) The Holy Father was convinced that when men begin to look upon each other as possessors of God-given rights they would become more aware of the brotherhood of all men, and that all men live in a world of moral values which must not be denied.

President Kennedy joined his voice to the voice of Pope John when, in his third State of the Union message, the late president stressed that the question of human rights was a moral issue.

"We are confronted with a moral issue. It is as old as the Scriptures and is as clear as the American Constitution." To deny any man his rights, whether in word or in deed or by sins of omission, is to deny human dignity and the God who granted this dignity and these rights to man.

Americans in the mid-twentieth century have been called upon by history to solve the problems which have arisen because of the denial of human rights. We have been challenged to recognize the moral issue involved in respecting the rights of all men. How we react to the denial of human rights in our own country is fraught with great consequence for the future of the entire world.

The United States is a testing ground for the world. The eyes of all men are upon us. The people of the United States are from all ethnic groups and represent all nationalities. If we can establish order and harmony in our country by a recognition of human rights and human dignity, our nation will become a sign of hope for the community of nations. If people of German, Irish, Jewish, African, Scandinavian and Mexican ancestry can live together as one people in our country, so also will it become evident to all nations that human unanimity is possible in the world at large.

The task that lies ahead of us is one of immense proportions. It demands that we exert every effort to construct our national society according to the patterns of justice and truth presented in the papal encyclicals.

As individuals we must achieve a consciousness of other human beings as children of God created in His image and likeness. We must become aware of the rights that God has bestowed upon all His children; we must become aware of our duties to respect these rights. We must be able to see beyond the color of a man's skin or the clothes he wears or the neighborhood in which he lives; we must be able to look beyond the surface appearances that we will be able to see the dignity each man possesses.

In all of our activities and associations with others we are called upon to practice the eternal truths outlined in *Pacem in Terris*. The Christian must engage himself in those activities that attempt to ransom human beings from environments which do not meet the requirements of human dignity. Slum clearance programs and similar welfare programs, sponsored either by private or governmental agencies, should receive our wholehearted support. Nor can we excuse ourselves from supporting these programs by saying that they are ineffective or unjust. We have an obligation to assist in making such programs more effective and just.

We are challenged to avoid using terms of scorn or slang words when speaking of people who are in some way different from us. "Nigger," "wop," "kike," and other such terms of opprobrium have no place in the Christian vocabulary. These designations represent an open violation to the dignity and rights of others and a rejection of the principles manifested in the papal encyclicals. The spiritual writers who compose lists of sins for model examinations of conscience should take special care to include these sins against human dignity in their lists.

The problem of recognizing human rights and working for the construction of a society in which the rights of all men are recognized is a problem we all must solve. It has been suggested by many spiritual leaders in the Church that social action groups be established in Catholic high schools and in every parish. Members of these groups could accomplish much if they met for the study of the papal social encyclicals and cooperated with each other for the implementation of the principles contained in the writings of the Holy Fathers.

If we are thoroughly imbued with the teaching of the Church on human rights, society cannot help but be better because we are present in society.

PROJECTS:

1. Select articles, editorials and passages from political speeches concerning human rights. Compare the ideas contained in these articles, editorials and magazines with the statements of Pope John.
2. Compare the first 38 paragraphs of *Pacem in Terris* with the Constitution and the Bill of Rights.
3. Make a list of your duties that correspond to the rights of other people around the world.
4. Find articles in the Catholic Press that indicate a growing awareness on the part of Catholics to honor the human rights of others.
5. Debate the following thesis: "American foreign aid is something due to underdeveloped countries by right of natural law."

DISCUSSION QUESTIONS:

1. Would it be feasible to begin a Christian Social Action group in your school or parish?
2. What are some of the violations of human rights you recognize in your home? In your school? In the world at large?
3. Discuss the morality of joining a neighborhood group that has as its main objective the restriction of the sale of homes to minority groups.
4. Discuss the means that might be employed to bring members of various ethnic groups into a closer harmony with each other.

The Church
and World Poverty

"I TELL YOU frankly: a rich man will find it difficult to enter the kingdom of heaven. I repeat, it is easier for a camel to pass through the eye of a needle than for a rich man to enter the kingdom of God." (Matthew 19:23f.)

Who is the rich man?

Most of us read the above passage with the pre-conceived notion that this teaching of Christ does not apply to us. When we think of rich men we think of pink Cadillac convertibles and fancy mansions. Besides, no need to worry about entering the kingdom of God. No need to fret about passing through the eye of a needle. We have been baptized. We *are* members of Christ's kingdom on earth. No need to pass an admissions test or an entrance exam for membership in the Church.

But the message of the gospel does apply to us, perhaps more than any other verse in sacred scripture.

Wealth and riches are relative things. We are rich in comparison with the people who will die today because of lack of nourishment. We are rich in comparison with the millions of people who live in sub-human squalor and who lack the very necessities of life. We Americans represent 6% of the world's population and we consume 40% of the world's goods. In the United States there are 790 people for every doctor; in Indonesia there are 71,000 people for each doctor. We waste enough food every day to feed the thousands who die each day of the direct or indirect effects of starvation. Sometimes statistics are cited in an attempt to boast; they are given here as an indictment. We are the "rich men" that Christ was talking about.

It is true, of course, that a person who has been baptized is a member of the Church. But formal membership in God's kingdom on earth is not a guarantee of personal goodness or eternal salvation. It is not an assurance we are *authentically* Christian. Many a traitor has waved his country's flag with unmatched vitality. Is it possible that many Christians today are waving the banner of the cross while betraying Christ's teachings in their daily lives?

The verses in Matthew's gospel about the rich man should disturb us profoundly — profoundly enough that we begin to look for ways of sharing our vast wealth with others: with those who retire to their gutter each night too sick to weep, too numb with hunger to whimper.

Poverty is a general term that can be used to designate many different situations. Poverty means many things, but above all else poverty means hunger.

Diplomats and world politicians, economists and scientists, technologists and clergymen—men from all walks of life—are beginning to become more and more concerned with world hunger. People who have weighed the evidences offered by the modern world agree that the greatest threat to humanity is not posed by ICBM's with nuclear warheads, but by the specter of world famine. Some experts have even predicted that unless something is done to provide food for millions of starving people, there is the danger that cannibalism will be practiced in the future and men will turn to savagery in many parts of the globe.

If this vision of world famine were merely the product of an unhealthy imagination, we could dismiss it immediately. But the vision and threat of famine is very real. Already various countries in the Orient are beginning to experience famine in massive proportions. If the dangers of famine were unavoidable, we could shut our eyes and declare, "What's the use!" But famine is not unavoidable. The human family possesses all the resources to vanquish this deadly foe of mankind. "Having discovered the atom and conquered outer space, our age needs such efforts in forging new paths leading to almost limitless horizons," wrote Pope John. (*Pacem in Terris*, Paragraph 156) Hunger *can* be destroyed and removed from the face of our planet.

Let us point out, by the way, that birth control is not and never was the answer to economic and social problems that breed poverty and hunger. The answer to poverty and hunger lies in the application of the principles of justice together with the technological and scientific discoveries that man has achieved and is capable of attaining in greater measure. There are more positive ways of dealing with our problems than birth control. Besides, it's too late now and has been too late for quite some time, to attempt to solve the problem of hunger by national campaigns for birth control. What we need are more positive approaches. As Pope Paul stated in his memorable address to the General Assembly of the United Nations: "You must strive to multiply bread so that it suffices for the tables of mankind, and not rather favor an artificial control of birth, which would be irrational, in order to diminish the number of guests at the banquet of life."

Hunger is but one segment of the vicious circle of poverty. When a nation becomes hungry and undernourished, that nation becomes sickly and debilitated. Those who are constantly sick and weak, the work force of a nation, are incapable of making technical and industrial advances. They are unable to employ modern methods of farming. Even if they had modern tractors and chemical fertilizers, the people's inability to work would prohibit agricultural advances. Without agricultural advances, there is not enough food. And without enough food, there is hunger. The economy becomes as sick as the people of the country and the gap between the rich nations and the poor nations widens all the more.

In Canada a farmer, using all the modern means of agriculture, can grow enough food to feed 450 people. In underdeveloped countries the farmer is lucky to grow enough food to feed four or five people. The situation will get worse unless something is done.

Pope John has outlined what must be done in *Mater et Magistra*. (Paragraphs 122-221)

The Holy Father was convinced that the fundamental question that arises everywhere in the world today is how to make agriculture more productive, and how to insure a sufficient labor force in non-urban areas. He concerns himself first with the duties of public authorities toward those who labor in farm areas.

"It is above all indispensable that great care be taken, especially by public authorities, to insure that the essential public services are adequately developed in rural areas: good roads, transportation, means of communication, drinking water, housing, health facilities, elementary education, technical and professional training, provision for the practice of religion and for recreation, and finally, a good supply of those products needed to insure that farm homes are furnished and equipped to be run on modern lines.

"Whenever such services, which are essential for a decent standard of living on the farm, are lacking to rural dwellers, socio-economic progress becomes almost impossible, or takes place too slowly." (Paragraph 127)

Government authorities must attempt to formulate wise and just agricultural policies (Paragraph 131) and taxes imposed should always "be proportionate to the capacity of the people to contribute." The Pope wisely noted that farm income flows in more slowly than industrial income and there is a greater necessity of accumulating capital savings by farmers. Those who are able to invest capital in agricultural enterprises are urged to do so, despite the fact that such investments do not normally yield a high rate of profit.

The sovereign pontiff also urges special credit agencies be set up to provide capital and credit for agricultural enterprises at a low rate of interest.

"In agriculture the creation of two forms of insurance seems essential: one covering agricultural produce, the other covering the farm labor force and their families." (Paragraph 135) "Systems of social insurance and social security can contribute effectively to the redistribution of national income according to the standards of justice and equity." (Paragraph 136)

The Holy Father also suggested that agricultural growth could be achieved by establishing industries and services which process farm products in rural areas. (Paragraph 142) Such enterprises as these would prevent rural areas from becoming "pockets of poverty." The Pope recommended that farm workers form systems of cooperatives and other organizations to protect the interests of the farmer. He urged farmers to become ever more interested in their mutual problems and "to take the initiative and play an active role in promoting their own economic advancement, social progress and cultural betterment." (Paragraph 144)

Above we used the term "pockets of poverty." Pope John noted in *Mater et Magistra* that some regions of a particular nation may suffer because of socio-economic inequalities. Public authorities, therefore, have the responsibility of formulating just and effective policies to eradicate all injustices in the socio-economic field. "But government action along these lines must always be justified by the demands of the common good." (Paragraph 151) Public authorities should encourage and assist private enterprise in attempting to contribute to the economic betterment of impoverished and backward areas. (Paragraph 152) In other words, we must employ the principle of subsidiarity (see pp. 40-41) in dealing with the various problems that prohibit economic growth in some sections of a country.

We are not as familiar with poverty and hunger in the United States as are some of the emerging nations of the modern world. Indeed, some of the most ancient cultures are now finding that they are beset by the monster of famine. While we in the United States have experienced a rapid rate of economic, agricultural and social growth, many other lands are in almost primitive stages of development. Our obligations toward the peoples of these lands are evident.

"The solidarity which binds all men and makes them members, in a sense, of the same family requires that nations enjoying an abundance of material goods should not remain indifferent to those nations whose citizens suffer from internal problems that result in poverty, hunger and an inability to enjoy even the more elementary human rights. This obligation is all the more urgent since, given the growing interdependence among nations, it is impossible to preserve a lasting and beneficial peace while glaring socio-economic inequalities persist among them." (Paragraph 157)

"Everyone is aware that some countries have a surplus of consumer goods—especially farm produce—while in other lands large segments of the population suffer from hunger and want. Justice and humanity demand, then, that the rich come to the aid of the poor. To destroy or to squander goods that other people need for survival goes against all canons of equity and human kindness." (Paragraph 161)

When we read in the papers of the billions of dollars the United States gives to other countries, we sometimes wonder if we are not doing more than is required to fulfill our obligations. Actually, what we give to other nations less fortunate than the United States is only a fraction of our *gross national product*. Using GNP as a base for comparison we may be surprised to discover that other countries are more generous than we in sharing material goods with others.

Not only must our assistance to developing countries become greater from the standpoint of dollars. It must become more effective. We must teach people to help themselves. This means we must offer assistance by way of scientific and technical training. The Holy Father noted in *Mater et Magistra* that assistance to developing nations was being given by the developed nations. But he also expressed the hope that "the wealthier nations will redouble their efforts to promote the scientific, technical and economic progress of the underdeveloped nations." (Paragraph 165)

It would be good for us to realize that it is "just good business" for the wealthier nations to help promote the economy of the developing nations. If foreign economies are sound, other nations will be able to purchase more goods from us. To put it in another way, by helping other countries to secure a standard of living that is just and humane, we are also creating markets abroad for our products.

All economists worthy of the name recognize that economics is world-wide in its scope. All of the nations of the world must advance together or they will not advance at all. What is right and just is also beneficial from the material standpoint. Universal prosperity is thinkable only in terms of justice.

Pope John cautioned the wealthy nations to avoid the temptation of making "colonies" out of developing nations. He explicitly stated that the wealthy nations, "when lending their help, must recognize and respect this individuality (of the developing nations) and take pains not to yield to the temptation of imposing their own way of life while aiding such nations." (Paragraph 170) The wealthy nations must "take care lest, while giving help to less developed nations, they turn the political situation that prevails there to their own profit or imperialistic aggrandizement." (Paragraph 171)

Our help to other nations must be a "no-strings-attached" type of help. Recent history shows the impracticality and futility of trying to "buy" other nations. Our assistance to the developing nations must be disinterested; it must not look to selfish interests.

The problem of world poverty and famine is a problem of such immense proportions that it can be solved only if all of the peoples of our planet cooperate with one another. It is a sad commentary upon humanity itself that so many dollars and rubles are being spent on weapons of war while so many people are dying from starvation. (Paragraph 204)

The sovereign pontiff wisely taught that nations must overcome their lack of trust. He also pointed out that this trust, a necessary prelude to cooperation among the nations, must be built upon the moral order. "Mutual trust among the heads of nations cannot stand firm and become deep-rooted without initial recognition of and respect for a just moral order from both sides. The moral order, however, cannot be built except on God. Cut off from God, it disintegrates." (Paragraphs 207-208)

It would be remiss of us, in any consideration of world poverty, to neglect to discuss what the basic attitude of the Christian should be in regard to the poor. So many times we hear that only the "deserving" poor should receive our assistance. The truth of the matter is that all men are deserving. Those people who have been reduced to laziness because of their environment are as equally deserving as the poor who have expended their energies in the fight against poverty. Even the so-called "undeserving" poor have rights and human dignity. Even these must be helped to become "deserving" and enthusiastic about their welfare.

Perhaps the Christian can best see what his attitude toward the poor should be in the light of Our Lord's description of the final judgment.

"When the Son of Man returns in His glory, and escorted by all the angels, He will seat Himself on a throne befitting His glory. All the nations will assemble in His presence, and He will part mankind into two groups just as a shepherd parts the sheep from the goats....

"Then the king will say to those at His right: 'Welcome, favored of my Father! Take possession of the kingdom prepared for you from the beginning of the world. For when I was hungry, you gave me to eat; when I was thirsty, you gave to me drink; when I was a stranger, you took me into your homes; when I was naked, you covered me; when I was in prison, you came to see me.' Then the saints will be surprised and say to him: 'Master, when did we see you hungry and feed you? or thirsty and give you to drink? And when did we see you a stranger and take you into our homes? or naked and cover you?'

"...In explanation the King will say to them: 'I tell you the plain truth, inasmuch as you did this to one of these least brethren of mine, you did it to me.'" (Matthew 25:31ff)

When we help and assist the poor of the world we are helping and assisting Christ Himself. The poor are in reality our *benefactors*. They make it possible for us to concretize and to actualize our love for Christ. The poor assist us by furnishing us with the opportunity of proving to ourselves and to the world that our love of God is something more than empty words. Our response to world poverty is a response to God. It is in measuring our response to the least of Christ's brethren that we are able to measure the meaning of our love for God.

PROJECTS:
1. Look in the New Testament and find several passages in which Our Lord talks about wealth and poverty.
2. Design a bulletin board display depicting the face of poverty in various countries of the world.
3. Write to your congressman and ask for available materials regarding world poverty and/or foreign aid.
4. Write an essay on the topic: "Helping the *Undeserving* Poor."
5. Make out a yearly budget for a man with a wife and four children who makes only 2,500 dollars a year.

DISCUSSION QUESTIONS:
1. In what ways are you "wealthy" as compared to the majority of the people in the world?
2. Why is it not unjust for a government to tax people who live in depressed agricultural sections less than people who live in commercial and industrial centers? Is it unjust?
3. Why is it not enough just to give food to impoverished nations?
4. "Foreign aid is nothing more than a massive hand-out that will accomplish no good in the long run." Do you agree with this statement?
5. Should the United States cut off economic aid to those countries which do not vote with us in the United Nations?

The Church
and the United Nations

ON JUNE 26, 1945, the United Nations Organization was formed by a gathering of representatives from 51 nations. The United Nations Organization has come a long way since its beginning in San Francisco more than 20 years ago. The number of nations represented in the United Nations has more than doubled and the services of the United Nations have become more and more complex.

Every high school student is familiar with the machinery and offices of the United Nations to a certain degree. We have all heard of the General Assembly and the Security Council. We know that UNICEF—the United Nations Children's Fund—accomplishes much good. Perhaps we have read about the Food and Agriculture Organization of the U.N., the World Health Organization and the Advisory Committee on the Peaceful Uses of Atomic Energy.

But what does the Church have to say about the United Nations?

Shortly after the U.N. was founded, and even to the present time, some individuals have condemned this organization. Critics of the U.N. base their objections to this international body either on arguments that our support of the U.N. is "unpatriotic" or on arguments that the U.N. is a "godless" organization dominated by the Communist conspiracy. "Get the U.S. out of the U.N. and the U.N. out of the U.S." is the rallying cry of a strong and dedicated minority of Americans today.

What directions have been given us by the Church regarding the U.N.? What is Catholic social doctrine concerning the U.N.?

First of all, we must not think that the Church has defined dogmatically what our attitude toward the U.N. must be. Just as a person can be a practicing Catholic and at the same time deny the apparitions at Fatima, a person can be a practicing Catholic and deny the usefulness and effectiveness of the U.N. A Catholic is not obliged by faith to accept the U.N. as a contributor toward peace nor is he obliged by faith to condemn the U.N. for being "godless." The Church has not officially put the stamp of approval or disapproval upon the United Nations.

The Holy Fathers have, of course, concerned themselves about the United Nations. And if we examine papal pronouncements carefully, we shall discover that the Holy Fathers look favorably toward the U.N. while at the same time encouraging this organization to become more worthy of the tasks it must face in the future.

Pope John explicitly praised a bureau of the United Nations in *Mater et Magistra*.

"...We must express Our warm approval of the work which the United Nations Food and Agricultural Organization (FAO) has been doing. This organization has as its special objective to promote fruitful accord among nations; to encourage the modernization of agriculture in underdeveloped nations; and to alleviate the sufferings of hunger-stricken peoples." (Paragraph 156)

Pope John commended the United Nations even more strongly in the encyclical *Pacem in Terris*.

"As is known, the United Nations was established on June 26, 1945, and to it there were subsequently added inter-governmental agencies with extensive tasks in the economic, social, cultural, educational and health fields. The United Nations has as its essential purpose the maintenance and consolidation of peace between peoples, fostering between them friendly relations based on the principles of equality, mutual respect and varied forms of co-operation in every sector of human endeavor.

"An act of the highest importance performed by the United Nations was the Universal Declaration of Human Rights, approved in the General Assembly on December 10, 1948. In the preamble of that declaration, the recognition and respect of those rights and respective liberties is proclaimed as an ideal to be pursued by all peoples and all countries.

"Some objections and reservations, We observed, were raised regarding certain points in the declaration, and rightly so. There is no doubt, however, that the document represents an important step on the path toward the juridico-political organization of the world community." (Paragraphs 142,143 and 144)

Certainly there are objections and reservations to the Declaration on Human Rights and even to the Charter of the U.N. God is not even mentioned in either of these documents. Nonetheless, the dignity of man is recognized and the objectives of the U.N. are objectives that every Christian can work for without compromising his beliefs. Pope John took a positive stance in regard to the United Nations and not a negative one. He chose to light a candle instead of cursing the darkness; to praise men for sincere efforts while instructing them that they must do more if they wish to accomplish the goal of peace among men.

"It is Our earnest prayer that the United Nations — in its structure and in its means — may become ever more equal to the magnitude and nobility of its tasks." (*Pacem in Terris,* Paragraph 145)

The historic visit of Pope Paul to the United Nations General Assembly did much to dispel the notion that Catholics should have a negative attitude toward the United Nations. The commendation of the United Nations given by Pope Paul leaves no doubts as to the attitude of the Church toward the U.N. Only an unthinking Catholic, or a Catholic who is rash and unwise, would insist on condemnations of the U.N. in the light of the Holy Father's address.

Pope Paul told the General Assembly that he came to bring a message to each of the members of the General Assembly.

"We might call our message a ratification, a solemn moral ratification of this lofty institution. This message comes from our historical experience. As 'an expert in humanity,' we bring to this organization the suffrage of our recent predecessors, that of the entire Catholic episcopate and our own, convinced as we are that this organization represents the obligatory path of modern civilization and of world peace.

"Gentlemen, you have performed and you continue to perform a great work: the education of mankind in the ways of peace. The United Nations is the great school where that education is imparted....

"Let unanimous trust in this institution grow, let its authority increase, and this aim (peace), will be secured."

The Holy Father encouraged the diplomats for the work they were doing. He also instructed them to remember that "...the edifice of modern civilization must be built upon spiritual principles which alone can, not only support it, but even illuminate and animate it."

While there is no *divinely revealed truth* we must accept about the United Nations, it is reasonable to conclude that the United Nations deserves our full support.

Sad to relate, even after the Pope's visit to the General Assembly some commentators, Catholics among them, continued to look at the United

Nations in a negative way. They told us, and are telling us today, that we cannot be true patriots if we support the United Nations.

True patriots are those who are committed to the principles of justice and truth promoted by their countries. A true patriot is not one who says: "My country, may she always be right, but my country right or wrong." This is the very absence of patriotism. No man who is content with unjust or deceitful practices executed by his country can lay claim to the virtue of patriotism. Authentic love for our country means that we take every precaution to protect our country from sponsoring anything evil or unjust, and that when evil or injustice is committed in the name of our country we rise up to denounce this evil and injustice.

At the root of much evil in the world today lies an inordinate lust for one's homeland that places national prestige above all else, even the moral order and laws of God. This inordinate lust for national interest, without a thought to matters of justice and the general welfare of humanity, is a vice that plagues much of the world today and creates mistrust among nations.

The Holy Fathers have consistently urged us to remember that we are members of one human family; that narrow national interests should not, and must not, destroy the universal common good.

"The unity of the human family has always existed because its members are human beings all equal by virtue of their natural dignity. Hence there will always exist the objective need to promote in sufficient measure the universal common good, that is, the common good of the entire human family." (*Pacem in Terris,* Paragraph 132)

The attitude of nationalism was perhaps necessary at one stage of human history. Nationalism helped unite peoples of one country in a common effort for economic and social progress. But what is needed today is a common effort for international economic, cultural and social progress.

The renowned Catholic economist Lady Jackson (Barbara Ward) has indicated that nationalism is but tribalism on a grand scale. In answering the question how nationalism had its beginnings she writes: "How, then, has it arisen? Some of its roots, for all its modernity, are very old indeed. They go back to what was for perhaps a hundred thousand years the basic social institution of mankind, the tribe. This system, which is still a living reality only in Africa and in parts of Asia, was once universal. All our societies have in some measure developed from the original tribal pattern and it undoubtedly foreshadows some of the characteristics of our latter-day full-blooded nationalism." (*Five Ideas that Change the World,* W.W. Norton Co., 1959).

We can excuse primitive tribesmen for their mistrust of other tribes which had different tribal practices and different cultural backgrounds. We cannot excuse modern man for his nationalism, his grand scale tribalism. We cannot excuse modern man when he puts his nation above the moral obligations he has in reference to other nations. What is demanded today for the very survival of humanity is close cooperation among all nations.

The Holy Fathers have not indicated that each nation must forsake its national sovereignty in favor of one universal super-nation. But the pontiffs have instructed us that we must come to a proper understanding of "sovereignty." In an address of Pope Pius XII to the fifth congress of Italian Jurists he had this to say:

"Sovereignty in the true sense means self-rule and exclusive competence concerning what has to be done and how it is done in regard to the affairs of a definite territory, always within the framework of international law, without however becoming dependent on the juridical system of any other state.

"Every state is immediately subject to international law. States which would lack this fullness of power, or whose independence of the power of any other state would not be guaranteed by international law, would not be sovereign.

"But no state could complain about a limitation of its sovereignty if it were denied the power of acting arbitrarily without regard for other states. Sovereignty is not the divinization of the state, or omnipotence of the state...."

The purpose of a world community of nations is not to deny national sovereignty; it is to "create on a world basis, an environment in which the public authorities of each political community, its citizens and intermediate associations, can carry out their tasks, fulfill their duties and exercise their rights with greater security." (*Pacem in Terris*, Paragraph 141)

If our love for our country is tempered with a love for justice and a recognition that all men belong to one human family, there is no danger of us falling into the evils of a narrow nationalism—an attitude that has been responsible for so many injustices in the course of human events and even wars. International cooperation alone, with the help of God, can prevent injustices and wars that have been the scourge of mankind for centuries.

When we examine the activities of the United Nations we can readily see why Pope John spoke so favorably of this institution and why Pope Paul was generous with his praise of the United Nations.

On the international level the United Nations helps the struggling and suffering masses of humanity attain economic justice and social stability. The Food and Agricultural Organization of the U.N. assists hungry nations in agricultural planning and promotes means by which famine-ridden countries can cope with starvation. The World Health Organization undertakes to relieve disease and to remedy illness on a world-wide scale. The Advisory Committee on the Peaceful Uses of Atomic Energy promotes the availability of atomic power for the economic and social growth of developing nations.

No wonder, then, that the Holy Fathers have encouraged the activities of the United Nations! And it can be said, without any danger of error, that each and every Catholic is called to support the work of the United Nations in the modern world. In the pastoral constitution on the Church in the Modern World of Vatican II we read: "Every day human interdependence grows more tightly drawn and spreads by degrees over the whole world." This is good. Human interdependence and international co-operation can lead mankind forward to even greater strides of progress, progress that is spiritual as well as material.

Appendix

THE UNITED NATIONS CHARTER

PREAMBLE

We the people of the United Nations

determined to save succeeding generations from the
scourge of war,

which twice in our lifetime has brought untold sorrow to
mankind,

and to reaffirm faith in fundamental human rights,

in the dignity and worth of the human person,

in the equal rights of men and women and of nations
large and small,

and to establish conditions under which justice and respect
for the obligations arising from treaties and other
sources of international law can be maintained,

and to promote social progress and better standards of life
in larger freedom.

And for these ends

to practice tolerance and live together in peace with one
another as good neighbors,

and to unite our strength to maintain international peace
and security,

and to ensure, by the acceptance of principles and the
institution of methods,

that armed force shall not be used,

save in common interest,

and to employ international machinery for the promotion of economic and social advancement of all peoples,

have resolved to combine our efforts to accomplish these aims.

PROJECTS

1. Make a chart showing the various offices and agencies of the United Nations, and how they are related to each other.
2. Outline an article in an encyclopedia concerning the United Nations.
3. Locate the various developing nations of the world on a map. Each student should select one of these countries and present a brief speech about this country.
4. Debate the following resolution: "Red China should be allowed admittance into the United Nations."
5. In what ways would you change the preamble of the United Nations charter to make it more acceptable to you as a Christian? Rewrite this preamble making suggested changes.

DISCUSSION QUESTIONS

1. What are the motives of those who attack the United Nations?
2. Is an organization necessarily "godless" because its charter does not refer directly to God?
3. How can the machinery of the United Nations be employed for the Christianization of world society?
4. Discuss the advantages and disadvantages of strong national feeling in the population of any country.
5. Describe some advantages of an international juridical order that would admit national sovereignty in its true sense and yet remain strong enough to assist the general welfare of all humanity.
6. Discuss the advantages and disadvantages of an international police force.

The Church
and the World

DURING THE COURSE of a high school retreat, a question box was passed around and the students were afforded the opportunity of asking the retreat master any question that came to their minds. The question box was filled quickly and the retreat master unfolded the first scrap of paper. He spent the entire time allotted for the answering of the questions on one question. The question was this: "Why did you become a priest? Was it because you hated the world?"

The priest began to answer the question with the statement, "I became a priest not because I hated the world, but because I love the world." The answer, we must admit, does not make too much sense without some explanation. To be sure, the priest's answer *could* even be thought of as an answer a secularist might give were he asked why he became a secularist. (Secularism, as we shall use the term in this chapter, is a way of life which denies any values beyond the values of this present world. In this sense, the secularist is also an implicit atheist.)

What did the priest mean when he said he *loved* the world? Is this the teaching of the Church regarding the world, that we must love it?

Before we can determine the attitude of the Church toward the world with any degree of accuracy, we must ask what is meant by the "world."

"World" has two opposing connotations. In other words, the term "world" can be used in two vastly different senses.

In one sense, a negative sense, the term "world" is used in the New Testament to indicate all those evil forces and influences which oppose the redemptive work of Christ; all those malicious negativities which contradict the promptings of the Holy Spirit and His work of sanctification. Thus does St. John warn us: "Do not love the world or what the world has to offer." (1 Jn. 2:15)

But "world" has another meaning. In a more positive sense "world" simply means the material universe that God brought forth from its own nothingness; the cosmos that God is continually creating by His creative act of love.

There have always been Christians who have understood this distinction of meanings in the term "world." There has always been a tradition of Christian humanism in the Church. Christian humanism is an outlook on the world by which the world is seen as a glorious sign of God's majesty and a manifestation of His love. Who can look at a rose in the springtime or the star-filled skies on a summer evening and not feel in his heart a marvelous admiration for the world?

Sad to say, there have also been Christians in ages past who have not understood the diverse meanings of "world" as it is used in the New Testament. Many individuals, in faulty but sincere conscience, have scorned the world totally. They emphasized the *eternal* aspects of salvation and completely ignored the *temporal* aspects of Christ's saving action. Their eyes were fixed exclusively on heaven; the problems and tribulations of planet earth did not attract their attention.

This over-emphasis on heaven and the neglect of earthly concerns has furnished the enemies of Christianity with much ammunition. They attack Christianity for being so concerned with the *celestial* future that the *terrestrial* future of man is not even considered. These enemies of Christianity, many of them in good faith, tell us that Christianity is completely other-worldly and is, therefore, disqualified to be a leaven of the social order. The enemies of Christianity point out the faults of *some* Christians and then proceed to condemn Christianity. An error of logic known as hasty generalization.

One of the most important documents of Vatican II is the pastoral constitution "The Church in the Modern World." This document ranks as one of the most important documents of the Council because it clears up many misunderstandings about the attitude of the Church toward the world.

The Church is certainly concerned about the eternal and celestial salvation of man. But this does not mean that the Church is unconcerned about the temporal and terrestrial future of man. In fact, the Church is keenly interested in the temporal needs of men and in the future of the city of man. The pastoral constitution on the Church in the Modern World explicitly and publicly witnesses the Church's desire to promote the success of the earthly endeavors of the human community.

Pope Paul, at the opening of the second session of Vatican II, has this to say about the world: "May the world know that the Church looks at it with profound understanding, with a sincere admiration, sincerely disposed, not to subjugate it but to serve it, not to depreciate it but to appreciate it, not to condemn it but to sustain and serve it." The Holy Father's statement is certainly in accord with another instruction of St. John: "So marked, indeed, has been God's love for the world that He gave His only-begotten Son...The fact is, God did not send the Son into the world to condemn the world. Not at all; the world is to be saved through Him." (Jn. 3:16-17)

Even more urgent than the question "What does the Church think about the world?" is this question: "What does the ordinary man of the world think of the world?" What is the outlook of the individual who is more concerned about this world than he is with heaven? The question is extremely difficult to answer. Modern man does not seem to have a well-defined set of feelings toward the world. When confronted with this question, most modern men find themselves incontestably confused.

Despite modern progress and invention many human beings are perplexed by the complexities of this world. At times the world appears to them to be an enchanting paradise; at other times the world takes on the semblance of a frightening place.

"Though mankind is stricken with wonder at its own discoveries and its power, it often raises anxious questions about the current trend of the world, about the place and role of man in the universe, about the meaning of its individual and collective strivings, and about the ultimate destiny of reality and of humanity." (*The Church in the Modern World*, Section 3)

The Church states her position about the world not merely as a matter of public record. The Church offers her evaluation of the world, and man's place in it, for man's welfare and as a service to anxious humanity. "The council brings to mankind light kindled from the Gospel, and puts at its disposal those saving resources which the Church herself, under the guidance of the Holy Spirit, receives from her Founder. For the human person deserves to be preserved; human society deserves to be renewed." (Section 3)

In addressing herself to the modern world the Church first of all enunciates the principle that the future of the world will be determined not by blind fate nor by a providential plan that destroys human freedom. The future will be shaped by men who freely respond to God's will. The future will be bright only if men use their freedom in accordance with God's designs for the future.

Only the proper use of human freedom will make a better world. This is especially true when we consider human relationships. The relationship that should exist between one man and another, regardless of nationality or political allegiance, is the relationship of love.

The Church tells us that all men possess a marvelous dignity; that all men are *lovable* by reason of the fact that all men have been created in the image and likeness of God. "The root reason for human dignity lies in man's call to communion with God. From the very circumstance of his origin man is already invited to converse with God. For man would not exist were he not created by God's love and constantly preserved by it; and he cannot live fully according to truth unless he freely acknowledges that love and devotes himself to his Creator." (Section 19)

Doctrines such as secularism and atheism, which reduce man to a mere cog in the cosmic machinery, must be rejected not only because they are in opposition to God, but also because they are subversive to humanity and radical denials of human dignity. All value systems which deny that man is made for conversation with God, ultimately bring man down to a sub-human level. These false doctrines represent a menace to religion and to the world itself.

"In her loyal devotion to God and men the Church has already repudiated, and cannot cease repudiating, sorrowfully but as firmly as possible, those poisonous doctrines and actions which contradict reason and the common experience of humanity, and dethrone man from his native excellence." (Section 21)

Certainly this repudiation of atheism does not mean that we are urged to hate atheists. Even atheists are made to the image and likeness of God and, therefore, we must respect them as persons who are also called to converse with God. Indeed, the Church instructs us to *communicate* with atheists and secularists for the betterment of the world.

"While rejecting atheism, root and branch, the Church sincerely professes that all men, believers and unbelievers alike, ought to work for the rightful betterment of this world in which all alike live; such an ideal cannot be realized, however, without sincere and prudent dialogue." (Section 21)

We are challenged by the Church to broaden our viewpoints and to work more energetically for the general welfare of all humanity. "Every day human interdependence grows more tightly drawn and spreads by degrees over the whole world.... Every social group must take account of the needs and legitimate aspirations of other groups, and even of the general welfare of the entire human family." (Section 26)

The Church commissions us to strive to achieve the proper development of culture. When we hear the word "culture" we are likely to think of long-hair music and impressionistic art. But culture is more than this. Culture is "everything whereby man develops and perfects his many bodily and spiritual qualities." (Section 53)

To work for the advance of culture means that we must work to establish educational opportunities for all men that they may be liberated from the "misery of ignorance." It means providing better health care for the underprivileged multitudes. It means striving for a betterment of the ordinary laborer's working conditions. It means reducing the burden of sub-human living conditions such as the slum areas in our own country.

Any energies we expend for the proper development of culture are energies that are directed toward liberation. We are called to liberate our fellowmen from all circumstances and conditions that prevent his proper development, spiritually as well as materially.

Justice demands that we do all in our power to help men who live in an atmosphere of political tyranny. The human spirit cannot grow when it is impeded and thwarted by tyrannies of any kind. The human spirit suffocates in the atmosphere of tyranny.

Justice also demands that we attempt to provide our fellow men with sufficient leisure time. Leisure time, properly utilized, is fundamental to cultural growth and development. There is a danger, of course, that leisure time will be wasted. That is why we are directed by the pastoral constitution on "The Church in the Modern World" to imbue all leisure activities with the Christian spirit.

"With the more or less generalized reduction of working hours, the leisure time of most men has increased. May this leisure be used properly to relax, to fortify the health of the soul and body through spontaneous study and activity, through tourism which refines man's character and enriches him with understanding of others, through sports activity which helps to preserve equilibrium of spirit even in the community, and to establish fraternal relations among men of all conditions, nations and races. Let Christians cooperate so that the cultural manifestations and collective activity of our time may be imbued with a human and a Christian spirit." (Section 61)

The secularist tells us that he loves the world. But in reality he does not love the world. Or he loves the world badly and not enough. The only true lover of the world and lover of humanity is the dedicated Christian. The Christian wishes the best for the world and for humanity. He is dissatisfied with the status quo. He works for the betterment of the world. And the Christian alone, because of his love for the world and the power of Christ, possesses what it takes to create a better world and renew humanity.

The Son of God came into the world to transform the world. Although Christ, in His glorified body, now reigns with the Father in heaven, He is present in the world in His Mystical Body. As Christians we are the extension and prolongation of Christ in human history. His work is our work. To paraphrase Father Teilhard de Chardin, we must take the whole world in our hands and pronounce over it the words of consecration: The message of the gospel of Jesus Christ.

PROJECTS:

1. Obtain a copy of the pastoral constitution "The Church in the Modern World." Point out five statements of that which hold special relevance to the modern world.
2. Make a mobile out of coat hangers, wire and cardboard symbols. At the center of the mobile depict a symbol of Christ. Around the central symbol of Christ depict various symbols of this world.
3. Plan an activity of service whereby your class or group assist a poor family by liberating them in some way from a cultural deprivation. E.g., take the children of this family for a trip to the park or a good movie.

DISCUSSION QUESTIONS

1. When the Christian says, "I love the world," how must he qualify this statement?
2. What do most non-Christians think about the ultimate meaning of the world?
3. In what ways do atheism and secularism pose a threat to the world and to humanity? Cite examples.
4. Concerning what matters might a Christian and an atheist engage in profitable dialogue?
5. How can the words of the gospel of Christ consecrate and transform the world?

The Church
and Progress

THOSE OF THE human family who
are yet relatively young, in their thirties or forties,
realize profoundly the great technological and
scientific advances that have been made in the
past twenty years or so. These advances have
been amazing and stupendous. Really, we run out
of descriptive adjectives for the miracles wrought
in recent times by technology and science.

In the field of communications we have tran-
sistor radios and television; in medicine we take
note of the heart-lung machines and scientific
victory over polio; in education we marvel at
closed circuit television and language labs. The
moon was once the sole province of poets and
lovers. In past generations song writers looked
at the moon to discover a word that rhymed with
June; today everyone looks at the moon and asks,
"When will we get there and what will it be like
to live on the moon?"

People are alive today who *remember* a time when there were no airplanes. And now we look forward to a time in the near future when gigantic jets will transport 500 passengers from New York to Los Angeles at 2000 miles per hour. Today a person does not need to be over 35 to remember an era before television. Today, when something important happens in Tokyo or London, the event is electronically translated into a picture and we *see* the event within seconds. Or should we say within a fraction of a second?

We could go on reciting the litany of technological and scientific advances, but such a recitation is not necessary. Anyone who is more sensitive than a beast or a vegetable is aware of *progress*. But *is* technological advance really progress?

When this writer was growing up there were no television sets. There were no jet airplanes or polio vaccines. But neither were there ICBM's and nuclear bombs.

What is progress? Can progress be described in terms of better automobiles and electric carving knives? Is technological and scientific improvement necessarily progress? The answer is no.

Most of us are realists enough to admit that for all the advances of technology and science, the world is not necessarily more advanced in *human terms*. The pastoral constitution of Vatican II, "The Church in the Modern World" noted:

"Today, the human race is involved in a new stage of history. Profound and rapid changes are spreading by degrees around the whole world.

Triggered by the intelligence and creative energies of man, these changes recoil upon him, upon his decisions and desires, both individual and collective, and upon his manner of thinking and acting with respect to things and to people....

"As happens in any crisis of growth, this transformation has brought serious difficulties in its wake. Thus while man extends his power in every direction, he does not always succeed in subjecting it to his own welfare." (Section 4)

Technological and scientific improvements do not constitute authentic human progress. These wondrous achievements can be employed by men for human progress. But they can also be used to thwart human progress. These advances in science and technology can assist men in liberating others from social ills, physical diseases and ignorance. *But they can also be used to destroy man.* Let us not think that the world will be saved solely by the scientist; let us not think that a better future can be provided by the technologist alone.

In the last century there were many men who were convinced that science alone would provide a heaven-on-earth for man. These naive optimists believed that there was some automatic law which insured an inevitable progress. Others went even further in describing the Utopia that was just around the corner of the new century. They envisioned a place where Science replaced God and the moral order. Others made a god out of economics and flatly predicted that man would enjoy paradise when the world was subjected to one type of economic system.

The naive and simple optimists of the last century did not take into account human freedom. They did not see that authentic progress must be defined in terms of a relationship of love that must exist between God and man, and among all men.

The arrogant prophets of the new world, a paradise without God, would have been surprised to learn that the twentieth century was to witness the two most devastating wars in the annals of human history.

The anti-God Utopians of the last century were militantly anti-God because they saw God and Heaven as notions that kept people from working in this world. We must admit that some preachers did counsel people to forget social ills and turn their gaze to the world beyond. But this was never the proclamation of Christianity.

Quite naturally the Church opposed any philosophy of progress that left God and the moral law out of the picture. But the Church did not oppose progress in its authentic sense. Christian humanists have always known that material advances, scientific enterprises and technological endeavors are not incompatible with Christian principles and Christian hopes for the future. This is something that was stressed in the document "The Church in the Modern World."

"...Far from thinking that the works produced by man's own talent and energy are in opposition to God's power, and that the rational creature exists as a kind of rival to the Creator, Christians are convinced that the triumphs of the human race are a sign of God's grace and the flowering of

His own mysterious design. For the greater man's power becomes, the farther his individual and community responsibility extends. Hence it is clear that men are not deterred by the Christian message from building up the world, or impelled to neglect the welfare of their fellows, but that they are rather more stringently bound to do these very things." (Section 34)

The time has passed when scientists and technologists were dedicated to the idea that scientific improvement alone brings about authentic human progress. Today the perceptive scientist realizes that man must be directed by a higher law in his use of scientific improvements. Realistic technologists have come to the conclusion that technology needs a spirit. Nothing brought this conviction home to these men with greater force than the dropping of the first atomic weapon and the destruction of Hiroshima. Ever since the time tens of thousands of Japanese were consumed in an atomic holocaust, scientists, technologists and millions of other people have been preoccupied with the ethical and moral considerations involved in technological improvement and advance.

Confronted with dangers of world destruction today, the diplomats and politicians approach scientific and technological questions with a sense of wonder, awe and not a little apprehension. Hopefully these feelings will lead them to outline programs for the proper use of these improvements for the benefit of all humanity.

The Council, in a brilliant passage contained in "The Church in the Modern World" has this to say:

"Human activity, to be sure, takes its significance from its relationship to man. Just as it proceeds from man, so it is ordered toward man. For
when a man works he not only alters things and
society, he develops himself as well. He learns
much, he cultivates his resources, he goes outside
of himself and beyond himself. Rightly understood, this kind of growth is of greater value than
any external riches which can be garnered. A man
is more precious for what he is than for what he
has. Similarly, all that men do to obtain greater
justice, wider brotherhood, a more humane disposition of social relationships has greater worth
than technical advances." (Section 35)

The Church, therefore, sees human progress
in terms of greater justice for all men, brotherhood among all peoples and an ever increasing
sense of "humaneness" in all men. In a word, the
Church measures all improvements against the
measuring stick of love. Whatever indicates a
greater spread of charity and growth of charity
over the planet earth is something that can be
called "human progress."

The guidelines for progress, in its true and
authentic sense, is the will of almighty God.

"...The norm of human activity is this: that
in accord with the divine plan and will, it har-
monize with the genuine good of the human race,
and that it allow men as individuals and as members of society to pursue their total vocation and
fulfill it." (Section 36)

Whatever meshes with the moral order and
serves God inevitably meshes with the good of
the human race and provides a sèrvice for man.

Whatever opposes God's law and the moral order cannot help but threaten the general welfare of all humanity.

It is interesting to note that the word "torah," the Hebrew word which indicates God's law, can be translated as "guidance." The commandments and the laws of God are not mere arbitrary restrictions of man's power and initiative. They are guidelines for genuine human progress. Man, individually and collectively, needs the direction of God's moral order for true progress. The author Rabelais once wrote: "Knowledge without a conscience brings ruin to the soul." We paraphrase Rabelais and bring him up-to-date by saying: "Technology without a soul brings destruction to humanity." The "soul" that technology must have, if there is to be human progress, must be a soul that is attuned to the laws of God.

Some people are asking a question with increasing frequency in our times. The question is this: "Is the Church relevant to the technological era?" We cannot blame people for asking this question. In the mid-twentieth century, when so many institutions and ideas are being challenged, it is only reasonable to expect that even the Church would be challenged by the casual observer.

The casual observer, who sees merely the surface of the Church, sometimes thinks that the Church stands in the way of progress and human activity. But the person who realizes what the Church really is; the person who meditates deeply on the meaning of the Church discovers that the Church is in the vanguard of authentic human progress. The Christian commitment demands that we become involved in working not only for the eternal salvation of all men, but also for the temporal well-being of all men.

Technological achievement that does not promote human dignity and human freedom over the entire world is a dubious achievement. We are called upon to employ science and technology as means of *serving* our fellow men. We serve our fellow men because we know that this is the best way we can meet Christ and serve God.

We are called upon to use technology and science in a spirit of brotherly love, and in the Spirit of Christ. Technology and science need to be inspired by Christian love if they are to become promoters of progress and not the means of ultimately destroying life on our globe.

"Is the Church relevant to the technological era?" Perhaps this question should be turned around. "Is technology relevant without Christ?" But even if we attempt to answer the question as it stands — "Is the Church relevant?" — we must answer in the affirmative.

The person who possesses a keen sense of history and who is aware of the dramatic changes taking place all around him; the person who sees beneath the surface of reality is almost forced to admit that the Church, Christianity, is perhaps the most relevant reality in the modern world. We would go so far as to maintain that to be anything but a fervent and active Christian in the modern world is to be a living irrelevancy. The modern world must learn to love or it will perish. Christianity is the message of God's love for man; the message which challenges men with the simple teaching: "Little children, love one another." The centrality of the message of love in Christian teaching cannot be disputed. Nor can it be disputed that above all else the world needs love if it wishes to progress. This core doctrine of Christianity is the only motivating force in the world today that is capable of producing "progress."

"A new commandment I give you: love one another; as I love you, so I want you, too, to love one another. By this token all the world must know that you are my disciples — by cherishing love for one another." (John 13:34-35)

We are not opposed to technological improvements and scientific advances. We affirm that these developments are necessary for progress while at the same time we affirm the necessity of Christian love and the moral order. We hope to attain the joys of heaven; no less do we hope that God's blessings come upon men on earth.

All of us would do well to repeat in our hearts and to become dedicated to the words spoken by Pope Paul. These words succinctly and surely sum up the Christian attitude toward progress:

"...May the day come on which the prodigious energies of progress will be employed to satisfy the world's hunger and to educate future generations, to bring remedies to the recurrent ills of mankind. And let there no longer be on this earth any of those deliberately caused and unprofitable sufferings due to systematic political and social oppression, to racial strife, to the contempt and restriction of the just freedom of conscience and of expression."

Our motto must be: "Progress, yes. But authentic progress. Human progress. Progress energized by the Holy Spirit of Christ."

PROJECTS
1. Make posters depicting one of the marvelous technological inventions of the last 50 years. Be ready to show how this invention can be employed by us for Christ and our neighbor.
2. Make another mobile. This time present symbols of technological and scientific achievements. Place a symbol of Christ as the center of the mobile.
3. Search a dictionary of quotations for references to progress. Discuss these quotations with your classmates.

DISCUSSION QUESTIONS
1. What world problems must be solved today to attain authentic progress? Give reasons for your answers.
2. Which is the most important problem that confronts man today? How will the solution of this problem bring about progress?
3. Discuss this statement and if you agree with it: "Progress is not inevitable. Progress or regression depends on human freedom."
4. Granted that there is such a thing as progress, what is the goal of progress? Where will it all end?
5. Discuss the possibility of the creation of a Christian Utopia. (Perhaps this discussion should be preceded by a report on the notion of "Utopia" and the Utopian ideas of the past.)

The Church
and Peace

ON APRIL 11, 1963, Pope John
XXIII promulgated his encyclical *Pacem in Terris*
(Peace on Earth). He addressed this encyclical
not only to Catholics, but to all men of good will.
The response on the part of world leaders and
political commentators was immediate and, for
the most part, favorable.

The opening paragraph of the encyclical ex-
presses the sum and substance of the entire document:

"Men of every age have most eagerly desired
peace on earth, but peace can be established and
strengthened only if the order set down by God
is conscientiously observed."

From time immemorial man has been bel-
ligerent and warlike. Individual has been at odds
with individual; tribe has been engaged with
tribe in bloodthirsty battles; nation has opposed

nation in struggles to the death. The pagan god Mars, although he is nothing more than a mythical diety, has reigned too long in human history.

The antagonism and hatred that lurks in the heart of man has its root in the sin of the first man. God created Adam. Adam became conscious of being a "self." But Adam was dissatisfied with his identity as a creature. He attempted to become "like unto God" in such a way that God's moral order was disturbed. Man, by his free choice, became separated and alienated from God. Man closed himself to God's influences and refused to open his being to the divine will.

Adam created a situation of alienation from God. The children of Adam, born into this situation, soon discovered that alienation from God meant also that man was alienated from man, and that man was a stranger to himself. It is this trinity of alienations that has been at the root of all battles and wars. When man made himself, by sin, a stranger to God, man also made himself a stranger to his fellow men. Man's sense of belonging to one human family was diminished and almost totally obscured. Other men took the appearance of aliens rather than neighbors and brothers.

Alienated from himself man did not understand his fears, his suspicions of others, his desires and motives. He reacted toward his fellow men, therefore, in brutal and sometimes monstrous ways. He made war.

Pope John knew that before men could enjoy the blessings of peace, they must become disalienated from God and from each other by con-

scientiously following the law (torah — guidance)
of God. It is a practical devotion to the law of God
that alone will move men to make peace.

"Peace," said St. Augustine, "is the tranquillity that comes from order." This order is not
an order imposed by force of arms. It is not a
massive regimentation. The order that creates
peace is "...an order grounded on truth, built on
justice and perfected by charity; an order made
effective by liberty." (*Pacem in Terris,* Paragraph
167) It is an order that must pervade the hearts of
men before it pervades and governs the human
society.

Peace means an ordered society, a commu-
nity of nations. Notice, we do not say that a *collectivity* of nations makes for peace. A collectivity
of peoples is created without regard for individual
rights. A community is formed when individuals
freely abide by the norms of justice and truth.

In pursuing peace and in attempting to establish a community of nations, we must make
every effort to open the channels of communication among all men.

"The bonds between States must be regulated by truth and justice. They must also be
strengthened by the active joining together of
minds and resources. This can be done coopera-
tively in many ways and in many fields, as is taking place today with profit in the economic,
social, political, cultural, health and athletic
spheres. The public authority of the nation does
not exist to contain its people within the bound-
aries of their own country. Rather it exists to
promote the national common good, which cannot

be divorced from the common good of the entire human family." (Paragraph 98)

"The international common good requires that every form of communication and exchange be promoted among the citizens and the various groupings within each State." (Paragraph 100)

It is not a sign of patriotism for a nation, in the name of national sovereignty, to isolate itself from other nations. With sincere dedication to truth and justice we must strive to communicate with all peoples. If the general welfare of humanity is not served, neither will the national interests of individual States be served.

The complexities of the modern world demand that we become more and more conscious of our membership in the human family. Just as the individual family finds happiness and tranquillity when all of the members of that family are happy, tranquil and communicative, so also will the family of man discover happiness and tranquillity when individual nations are tranquil, happy and communicative.

If men truly followed God's laws and respected one another as members of the same human family, they would not stockpile weapons of destruction. Weapons are always a symbol of mistrust.

We do not mean to indicate that stockpiles of nuclear weapons are unnecessary to prevent aggression and war. Indeed, some people are of the opinion that massive stockpiles of nuclear arms have prevented the outbreak of major wars. Weapons may contribute something to the absence of major wars, but we must remember that the absence of war is not peace.

Bombers in the skyways and missiles aimed at national heartlands can never be more than a temporary deterrent to the outbreak of a major war. Gradually we must learn to do without nuclear arms. Even in the present situation we have great fears and disorders in the world. These fears can never be a basis for a lasting peace; these disorders can never be resolved unless all nations are willing to repudiate war as a means of achieving their objectives.

"All must realize that it is not possible to stop the arms race, to reduce the present supply of arms or—and this is the main point—to abolish arms altogether unless the disarmament process is complete and thorough and unless all cooperate sincerely to banish from the minds of men both fear and the anxious expectation of war. This requires that the grounds on which our present peace depends be replaced by the fundamental principle that the true and solid peace of nations can be found not in equality of arms but solely in mutual trust. We believe that this objective can be brought to pass, for it is not only required by right reason, but also eminently desirable and abundantly productive of good." (Paragraph 113)

If we wish to achieve a true and lasting peace, we must be ready to take the calculated risk of trusting our fellow men. And they who share with us the face of our planet, but who disagree with us in other matters, must be ready to take the calculated risk of trusting us. The absence of war is a reality achieved only by fear; peace, in the most proper sense of the word, can be achieved only through trust and disarmament.

In his address to the United Nations Assembly, Pope Paul made it clear that disarmament must be the first concern of modern man.

"Peace, as you know, is not built up only by means of politics, by the balance of forces and of interests. It is constructed with the mind, with ideas, with works of peace. You labor in this great construction. But you are still at the beginning of your task. Will the world ever succeed in changing that selfish and bellicose mentality which, up to now, has been interwoven with so much of its history? It is hard to foresee. But it is easy to affirm that it is toward that new history, a peaceful, truly human, history, as promised by God to men of good will, that we must resolutely march. The roads thereto are already well marked out for you; and the first is that of disarmament."

Let us suppose that the nations of the world will be successful in achieving an effective disarmament. How, then, will peace loving peoples be able to thwart aggression and maintain order? How will the community of nations be able to deal with threats to peace and order on the part of individual nations who are warlike?

The relationships which exist among all of the nations of the world must be based on international law. That law must be supported and sanctioned by some sort of permanent international police force. In order to make international law effective, it must be proclaimed by a representative governing body of all the nations of the world. We should not become apprehensive about the thought of world government. World government, in some form, appears to be the only

answer to the crucial political, social and economic problems of the present time.

Any world government, of course, would be
bound by the principle of subsidiarity and would
be required to recognize individual national sovereignty, insofar as individual national sovereignty did not adversely affect international harmony
and order.

Pope John outlined the rules for a world
authority in *Pacem in Terris.*

"...The universal public authority must have
as a prime objective the recognition, respect,
protection and promotion of the rights of the human person. This can be attained either by direct
action of the general authority, if conditions
warrant, or by creating on a world scale an environment in which the public authorities of individual States can more easily carry out their own
responsibilities in this regard." (Paragraph 139)

"Just as within each State the relations of
individual citizens, families, and organizations
with government should be regulated by the principle of subsidiarity, so too the relations between
the public authority of each State and the universal public authority should be governed by the
same principle. This universal authority is to consider and to solve economic, social, political, and
cultural problems springing from the international common good. We refer here to those problems which because of their gravity, extent, and
urgency are too difficult for the individual States
to handle successfully."(Paragraph 140)

Shortly after the Holy Father discussed a
universal world authority, he gave his approbation to the United Nations (Paragraphs 142-145).

While this approbation is a qualified approbation, there is no doubt that the Pope saw the United Nations as an effective international structure for the community of nations. "We ardently desire that the United Nations be increasingly able to adapt its structure and means to the magnitude and nobility of its tasks." (Paragraph 145).

But what can the individual Christian do to promote peace? What can he do besides supporting the United Nations and divesting himself of the attitudes of tribalism?

After His resurrection from the dead, Our Lord entered the upper room, the doors being locked, and appeared to His apostles. "Peace be to you," said Our Lord. "As the Father has made me His ambassador, so I am making you my ambassadors." (John 20:21)

It is by being an ambassador of Christ to others, by "breaking in" upon the lives of others with the message of Christ, that the individual Christian can work for peace in the world. This "breaking in" is accomplished not only by what we say, but also by *what we do* and *by what we are*. At the level of individual relationships we must be signs of Christ, the Prince of Peace. We must love our neighbor, even as Christ has loved us.

We have no way of knowing what the future holds in store for us. Like Abraham we must push off into the mists of the future not knowing where the road of time will take us, possessing only a faith and confidence in God, a love of God and neighbor. As we travel history's road we can take courage in the fact that our God is the God of history; the God of history's twistings and turnings. And with His help we can be sure that our presence in the world, if it is a truly Christian presence, will direct the current of human events toward peace on earth.

PROJECTS:

1. Make a list of the passages in the Mass in which the word peace is mentioned.
2. Make a list of the references to peace in the gospels.
3. Employing the above lists, write a brief essay on peace.
4. Conduct a meeting of the United Nations General Assembly. Each student should represent a different nation.

DISCUSSION QUESTIONS:

1. In your opinion, what practical steps can the nations of the world take to achieve peace?
2. What are the differences between a universal collectivity of peoples and a universal community?
3. Discuss the possibility of the ultimate domination of the peoples of the world by an international police force. Under what regulations would such a police force exist to prevent the use of this force for purposes of military conquest?
4. Why are missionaries effective agents of world peace?
5. How can the high school student become an agent for world peace in his local community?

The Development
of Peoples

IN THE PREVIOUS chapters we
have considered the social doctrines of the
Church according to a thematic scheme. That is,
we discussed "The Church and Society," "The
Church and Capitalism," "The Church and Communism," etc. In this chapter we are going to sum
up most of the themes we have already considered by studying an abridgement of the most recent social encyclical of Pope Paul. On Easter
Sunday, 1967, Pope Paul officially signed the encyclical *Populorum Progressio* (Development of
Peoples). In part, here is what the Holy Father
wrote:

The development of peoples has the
Church's close attention, particularly the development of those peoples who are striving to es-
cape from hunger, misery, endemic diseases and
ignorance; of those who are looking for a wider

share in the benefits of civilization and a more active improvement of their human qualities; of those who are aiming purposefully at their complete fulfillment....

Today the principal fact that we must all recognize is that the social question has become world-wide...Today the peoples in hunger are making a dramatic appeal to the peoples blessed with abundance. The Church shudders at this cry of anguish and calls each one to give a loving response of charity to his brother's cry for help....

THE HOPES OF MEN

Freedom from misery, the greater assurance of finding subsistence, health and fixed employment; an increased share of responsibility without oppression of any kind and in security from situations that do violence to their dignity as men; better education—in brief, to seek to do more, know more and have more in order to be more: that is what men aspire to know when a greater number of them are condemned to live in conditions that make this lawful desire illusory. Besides, peoples who have recently gained national independence experience the need to add to this political freedom a fitting autonomous growth, social as well as economic, in order to assure their citizens of a full human enhancement and to take their rightful place with other nations.

COLONIALISM

Though insufficient for the immensity and urgency of the task, the means inherited from the past are not lacking. It must certainly be recognized that colonizing powers have often furthered their own interests, power or glory, and that their departure has sometimes left a precarious economy...Yet while recognizing the damage done by a certain type of colonialism and its consequences, one must at the same time acknowledge the qualities and achievement of colonizers who brought their science and technical knowledge and left beneficial results of their presence in so many underprivileged regions....

MISSIONARIES

True to the teaching and example of her divine Founder, who cited the preaching of the Gospel to the poor as a sign of His mission, the Church has never failed to foster the human progress of the nations to which she brings faith in Christ. Her missionaries have built, not only churches, but also hostels and hospitals, schools and universities. Teaching the local population the means of deriving the best advantages from their natural resources, missionaries have often protected them from the greed of foreigners. Without doubt their work, inasmuch as it was human, was not perfect, and sometimes the announcement of the authentic Gospel message was infiltrated by many ways of thinking and acting which were characteristic of their home countries. But the missionaries were also able to develop and foster local institutions. In many a region they were the pioneers in material progress as well as in cultural advancement.

The Church and the World

However, local and individual undertakings are no longer enough. The present situation of the world demands concerted action based on a clear vision of all economic, social, cultural and spiritual aspects. Experienced in human affairs, the Church, without attempting to interfere in any way in the politics of states, "seeks but a solitary goal; to carry forward the work of Christ Himself under the lead of the befriending Spirit. And Christ entered this world to give witness to the truth, to rescue and not sit in judgment, to serve and not to be served." Founded to establish on earth the kingdom of heaven and not to conquer any earthly power, the Church clearly states that the two realms are distinct, just as the two powers, ecclesiastical and civil, are supreme, each in its own domain. But, since the Church lives in history, she ought to "scrutinize the signs of the times and interpret them in the light of the Gospel." Sharing the noblest aspirations of men and suffering when she sees them not satisfied, she wishes to help them attain their full flowering, and that is why she offers men what she possesses as her characteristic attribute: a global vision of man and of the human race.

The Christian Notion of Development

Development cannot be limited to mere economic growth. In order to be authentic, it must be complete: integral, that is, it has to promote the good of every man and of the whole man.... In the design of God, every man is called to develop

and fulfill himself, for every life is a vocation....
Endowed with intelligence and freedom, he is
responsible for his fulfillment as he is for his salvation. He is aided, or sometimes impeded, by
those who educate him and those with whom he
lives, but each one remains, whatever be these influences affecting him, the principal agent of his
own success or failure....

...This self-fulfillment is not something op-
tional. Just as the whole of creation is ordained to
its Creator, so spiritual beings should of their own
accord orientate their lives to God, the first truth
and the supreme good....

Communal Responsibility

But each man is a member of society. He is
part of the whole of mankind. It is not just certain
individuals, but all men who are called to this
fullness of development. Civilizations are born,
develop and die. But humanity is advancing along
the path of history like the waves of a rising tide
encroaching gradually on the shore. We have inherited from past generations, and we have bene-
fited from the work of our contemporaries: for this
reason we have obligations toward all, and we
cannot refuse to interest ourselves in those who
will come after us to enlarge the human family.
The reality of human solidarity, which is a benefit
to us, also imposes a duty.

Scale of Values

This personal and communal development
would be threatened if the true scale of values
were undermined. The desire for necessities is

legitimate, and work undertaken to obtain them is a duty: "If any man will not work, neither let him eat." But the acquiring of temporal goods can lead to greed, to the insatiable desire for more, and can make increased power a tempting objective. Individuals, families and nations can be overcome by avarice, be they poor or rich, and all can fall victim to a stifling materialism. Increased possession is not the ultimate goal of nations nor of individuals....

PROPERTY

"If someone who has the riches of this world sees his brother in need and closes his heart to him, how does the love of God abide in him?" It is well known how strong were the words used by the Fathers of the Church to describe the proper attitude of persons who possess anything toward persons in need. To quote St. Ambrose: "You are not making a gift of your possessions to the poor person. You are handing over to him what is his. For what has been given in common for the use of all, you have arrogated to yourself. The world is given to all, and not only to the rich." That is, private property does not constitute for anyone an absolute and unconditioned right. No one is justified in keeping for his exclusive use what he does not need, when others lack necessities....

LIBERAL CAPITALISM

...It is unfortunate that...a system has been constructed which considers profit as the key motive for economic progress, competition as the supreme law of economics, and private ownership of the means of production as an absolute right that has no limits and carries no corresponding social obligation. This unchecked liberalism leads to dictatorship rightly denounced by Pius XI as producing "the international imperialism of money." One cannot condemn such abuses too strongly by solemnly recalling once again that the economy is at the service of man. But if it is true that a type of capitalism has been the source of excessive suffering, injustices and fratricidal conflicts whose effects still persist, it would also be wrong to attribute to industrialization itself evils that belong to the woeful system which accompanied it. On the contrary one must recognize in all justice the irreplaceable contribution made by the organization of labor and industry to what development has accomplished.

WORK

Similarly with work: while it can sometimes be given exaggerated significance, it is for all something willed and blessed by God. Man created to His image "must cooperate with his Creator in the perfecting of creation and communicate to the earth the spiritual imprint he himself has received." God who has endowed man with intelligence, imagination and sensitivity, has also given him the means of completing His work in a certain way: whether he be artist or craftsman, engaged in management, industry or agriculture, everyone who works is a creator. Bent over a material that resists his efforts, a man by his work gives his imprint to it, acquiring, as he does so, perseverance, skill and a spirit of invention. Further, when work is done in common, when hope, hardship, ambition and joy are shared, it brings together and more firmly unites the wills, minds and hearts of men: in its accomplishment, men find themselves to be brothers.

Work of course can have contrary effects, for it promises money, pleasure and power, invites some to selfishness, others to revolt; it also develops professional awareness, sense of duty and charity to one's neighbor. When it is more scientific and better organized, there is a risk of it dehumanizing those who perform it, by making them its servants, for work is human only if it remains intelligent and free....

THE EVIL OF VIOLENCE

There are certainly situations whose injustice cries to heaven. When whole populations destitute of necessities live in a state of dependence barring them from all initiative and responsibility, and all opportunity to advance culturally and share in social and political life, recourse to violence, as a means to right these wrongs to human dignity, is a grave temptation.

We know, however, that a revolutionary uprising—save where there is manifest, longstanding tyranny which would do great damage to fundamental personal rights and dangerous harm to the common good of the country—produces new injustices, throws more elements out of balance and brings on new disasters. A real evil should not be fought against at the cost of greater misery.

We want to be clearly understood: the present situation must be faced with courage and the injustices linked with it must be fought against and overcome. Development demands bold transformations, innovations that go deep. Urgent reforms should be undertaken without delay. It is for each one to take his share in them with generosity, particularly those whose education, position and opportunities afford them wide scope for action....

PROGRAMS FOR REFORM

Individual initiative alone and the mere free play of competition could never assure successful development. One must avoid the risk of increasing still more the wealth of the rich, and the dominion of the strong, while leaving the poor in their misery and adding to the servitude of the oppressed. Hence programs are necessary in order "to encourage, stimulate, coordinate, supplement and integrate" the activity of individuals and of intermediary bodies. It pertains to the public authorities to choose, even to lay down the objectives to be pursued, the ends to be achieved, and the means for attaining these, and it is for them to stimulate all the forces engaged in this common activity. But let them take care to associate private initiative and intermediary bodies with this work. They will thus avoid the danger of complete collectivization or of arbitrary planning, which, by denying liberty, would prevent the exercise of the fundamental rights of the human person....

WHAT IS NEEDED: A COMPLETE HUMANISM

What must be aimed at is complete humanism. And what is that if not the fully-rounded development of the whole man and of all men? A humanism closed in on itself, and not open to the values of the spirit and to God who is their source, could achieve apparent success. True, man can organize the world apart from God, but "without God man can organize it in the end only to man's detriment. An isolated humanism is an inhuman humanism." There is no true humanism but that which is open to the Absolute and is conscious of a vocation which gives human life its true meaning. Far from being the ultimate measure of all things, man can only realize himself by reaching beyond himself. As Pascal has said so well: "Man infinitely surpasses man."

THE SOLIDARITY OF ALL HUMANITY

There can be no progress toward the complete development of man without the simultaneous development of all humanity in the spirit of solidarity. As we said at Bombay: "Man must meet man, nation meet nation, as brothers and sisters, as children of God. In this mutual understanding and friendship, in this sacred communion, we must also begin to work together to build the common future of the human race." We also suggested a search for concrete and practical ways of organization and cooperation, so that all available resources be pooled and thus a true communion among all nations be achieved.

BROTHERHOOD OF PEOPLES

This duty is the concern especially of better-off nations. Their obligations stem from a brotherhood that is at once human and supernatural, and take on a threefold aspect: the duty of human solidarity—the aid that the rich nations must give to developing countries; the duty of social justice—the rectification of inequitable trade relations between powerful nations and weak nations; the duty of universal charity—the effort to bring about a world that is more human toward all men, where all will be able to give and receive, without one group making progress at the expense of another. The question is urgent for on it depends the future of the civilization of the world.

HELP FOR THE HUNGRY

"If a brother or a sister be naked," says St. James, "if they lack their daily nourishment, and one of you says to them: 'Go in peace, be warmed and be filled,' without giving them what is necessary for the body, what good does it do?" Today no one can be ignorant any longer of the fact that in whole continents countless men and women are ravished by hunger, countless numbers of children are undernourished, so that many of them die in infancy, while the physical growth and mental development of many others are retarded and as a result whole regions are condemned to the most depressing despondency....

The campaign against hunger being carried on by the Food and Agriculture Organization (FAO) and encouraged by the Holy See, has been generously supported. Our Caritas International is at work everywhere....

But neither all this nor the private and public funds that have been invested, nor the gifts and loans that have been made, can suffice. It is not just a matter of eliminating hunger, nor even of reducing poverty. The struggle against destitution, though urgent and necessary, is not enough. It is a question rather of building a world where every man, no matter what his race, religion or nationality, can live a fully human life, freed from servitude imposed on him by other men or by natural forces over which he has no control; a world where freedom is not an empty word and where the poor man Lazarus can sit down at the same table with the rich man. This demands great generosity, much sacrifice and unceasing effort on the part of the rich man. Let each one examine his conscience, a conscience that conveys a new message for our times. Is he prepared to support out of his own pocket words and undertakings organized in favor of the most destitute? Is he ready to pay higher taxes so that the public authorities can intensify their efforts in favor of development? Is he ready to pay a higher price for imported goods so that the producer may be more justly rewarded? Or to leave his country, if necessary and if he is young, in order to assist in this development of the young nations?

SUPERFLUOUS WEALTH

The same duty of solidarity that rests on individuals exists also for nations.... We must repeat once more that the superfluous wealth of the rich countries should be placed at the service of poor nations. The rule which up to now held good for the benefit of those nearest to us, must today be applied to all the needy of the world. Besides, the rich will be the first to benefit as a result. Otherwise their continued greed will certainly call down upon them the judgment of God and the wrath of the poor, with consequences no one can foretell. If today's flourishing civilizations remain selfishly wrapped up in themselves, they could easily place their highest values in jeopardy, sacrificing their will to be great to the desire to possess more....

WORLD FUND

At Bombay we called for the establishment of a great World Fund, to be made up of part of the money spent on arms, to relieve the most destitute of this world. What is true of the immediate struggle against want, holds good also when there is a question of development. Only worldwide collaboration, of which a common fund would be both means and symbol, will succeed in overcoming vain rivalries and in establishing a fruitful and peaceful exchange between peoples.

There is certainly no need to do away with bilateral and multilateral agreements: they allow ties of dependence and feelings of bitterness, left over from the era of colonialism, to yield place to the happier relationship of friendship, based on a footing of constitutional and political equality. However, if they were to be fitted into the framework of a worldwide collaboration, they would be beyond all suspicion, and as a result there would be less distrust on the part of the receiving nations. These would have less cause for fearing that, under the cloak of financial aid or technical assistance, there lurk certain manifestations of what has come to be called neo-colonialism, in the form of political pressures and economic suzerainty aimed at maintaining or acquiring complete dominance....

Obstacles to World Unity

Among...obstacles which are opposed to the formation of a world which is more just and which is better organized toward a universal solidarity, we wish to speak of nationalism and racism. It is only natural that communities which have recently reached their political independence should be jealous of a national unity which is still fragile, and that they should strive to protect it. Likewise, it is to be expected that nations endowed with an ancient culture should be proud of the patrimony which their history has bequeathed to them. But these legitimate feelings should be ennobled by that universal charity which embraces the entire human family. Nationalism isolates people from their true good. It would be especially harmful where the weakness of national economies demands rather the pooling of efforts, of knowledge and of funds, in order to implement programs of development and to increase commercial and cultural exchange.

Racism

Racism is not the exclusive lot of young nations, where sometimes it hides beneath the rivalries of clans and political parties, with heavy losses for justice and at the risk of civil war. During the colonial period it often flared up between the colonists and the indigenous population, and stood in the way of mutually profitable understanding, often giving rise to bitterness in the wake of genuine injustices. It is still an obstacle to collaboration among disadvantaged nations and a cause of division and hatred within countries whenever individuals and families see the inviolable rights of the human person held in scorn, as they themselves are unjustly subjected to a regime of discrimination because of their race or color....

BUILDING A BETTER WORLD

World unity, ever more effective, should allow all peoples to become the artisans of their destiny. The past has too often been characterized by relationships of violence between nations; may the day dawn when international relationships will be marked with the stamp of mutual respect and friendship, of interdependence in collaboration, the betterment of all seen as the responsibility of each individual....

The world is sick. Its illness consists less in the unproductive monopolization of resources by a small number of men than in the lack of brotherhood among individuals and peoples....

DIALOGUE AND BROTHERHOOD

Between civilizations, as between persons, sincere dialogue indeed creates brotherhood. The work of development will draw nations together in the attainment of goals pursued with a common effort if all…are inspired by brotherly love and moved by a sincere desire to build a civilization founded on world solidarity. A dialogue based on man, and not on commodities or technical skills, will then begin. It will be fruitful if it brings to the peoples who benefit from it the means of self-betterment and spiritual growth, if the technicians act as educators, and if the instruction imparted is characterized by so lofty a spiritual and moral tone that it guarantees not merely economic, but human development….

APPEAL TO YOUTH

Many young people have already responded with warmth and enthusiasm to the appeal of Pius XII for lay missionaries. Many also are those who have spontaneously put themselves at the disposition of official or private organizations which are collaborating with developing nations. We are pleased to learn that in certain nations "military service" can be partially accomplished by doing "social service"…. We bless these undertakings and the good will which inspires them.

May all those who wish to belong to Christ hear His appeal: "I was hungry and you gave me to eat, thirsty and you gave me to drink, a stranger and you took me in, naked and you clothed me, sick and you visited me, a prisoner and you came to see me." No one can remain indifferent to the lot of his brothers who are still buried in wretchedness and victims of insecurity, slaves of ignorance. Like the heart of Christ, the heart of the Christian must sympathize with this misery: "I have pity on the multitudes."

A WORLD AUTHORITY

...International collaboration on a worldwide scale requires institutions that will prepare, coordinate and direct it, until finally there is established an order of justice which is universally recognized. With all our heart, we encourage these organizations which have undertaken this collaboration for the development of the peoples of the world, and our wish is that they grow in prestige and authority. "Your vocation," as we said to the representatives of the United Nations in New York, "is to bring not some people, but all peoples to treat each other as brothers.... Who does not see the necessity of thus establishing progressively a world authority, capable of acting effectively in the juridical and political sectors."

Some would consider such hopes utopian. It may be that these persons are not realistic enough, and that they have not perceived the dynamism of a world which desires to live more fraternally—a world which, in spite of its ignorance, its mistakes and even its sins, its relapses into barbarism and its wanderings far from the road of salvation, is, even unawares, taking slow but sure steps toward its Creator. This road toward a greater humanity requires effort and sacrifice; but suffering itself, accepted for the love of our brethren, favors the progress of the entire human family. Christians know that union with the sacrifice of our Savior contributes to the building up of the Body of Christ in its plenitude: the assembled people of God.

We are united in this progress toward God. We have desired to remind all men how crucial is the present moment, how urgent the work to be done. The hour for action has now sounded. At stake are the survival of so many innocent children and, for so many families overcome by misery, the access to conditions fit for human beings; at stake are the peace of the world and the future of civilization. It is a time for all men and all peoples to face up to their responsibilities....

PROJECTS

1. If there is a college near-by with foreign exchange students, investigate the possibility of inviting one of these students to your class to talk about the needs of his country.
2. Write to the Peace Corps in Washington and ask them to send you information about this organization. Find out if the Papal Volunteers have an office in your diocese. Write to this office for information concerning the work of the Papal Volunteers.
3. Make a list of statements from the documents of Catholic social doctrine, including *Populorum Progressio*, to show the basic consistency in the development of the Church's social teaching. Limit yourself to a particular theme. E.g., "Brotherhood," "Human Rights," "Wealth," etc.
4. Pretend you have been commissioned to write a thirty second television "commercial" for the poor of the world. What would you show? What statements from *Populorum Progressio* would you use?

DISCUSSION QUESTIONS:
1. Discuss what is entailed in the Christian notion of "development" and "progress." Is development authentic if it is restricted only to the economic aspects of life?

2. What is the attitude of most Americans toward their personal wealth? Is this attitude, in your opinion, similar to the attitude encouraged by the Holy Father?
3. In the light of the Holy Father's statement on violence, discuss the value of violent revolution as a means remedying social evil.
4. Why does the Pope deem it necessary to have a world authority to insure fruitful world collaboration?
5. In what ways does *Populorum Progressio* represent a development of Catholic social doctrine over and beyond previous statements of the Holy Fathers?

FOR FURTHER
READING AND DISCUSSION

A PAMPHLET LIBRARY ON THE SOCIAL QUESTION

Condition of the Working Classes POPE LEO XIII 25c
Atheistic Communism POPE PIUS XI 25c
Social Reconstruction POPE PIUS XI 25c
Function of the State in the Modern World POPE PIUS XII 25c
Mater et Magistra POPE JOHN XXIII 25c
Pacem in Terris POPE JOHN XXIII 25c
The Development of Peoples POPE PAUL VI 25c

SIXTEEN DOCUMENTS OF VATICAN II a paperback edition of the official texts of all the documents of the Second Vatican Council complete with **footnotes** and topic index. Enriched by **commentaries** on each document by renowned Council Fathers. 760 pages; $1.25

THE CHRIST OF VATICAN II All in the Words of the Second Vatican Council. COMPILED BY THE DAUGHTERS OF ST. PAUL. To a world that has in a sense lost a consciousness of things divine, and where a "death of God" theology is in vogue, the Second Vatican Council presented a vivid and vibrant profile of Christ the Lord.

Cloth $2.00; Paper $1.00

THE CATECHISM OF MODERN MAN COMPILED BY A GROUP OF SPECIALISTS. The Catholic Faith as the Second Vatican Council presented it to the world. Avoids the question and answer method. Enriched with topic index, discussion questions and suggestions for further reading. 600 pages; Cloth $5.00; Paper $4.00

FAITH — RESPONSE TO THE DIALOGUE OF GOD POPE PAUL VI. COMPILED BY THE DAUGHTERS OF ST. PAUL. The Pope speaks to the modern world on Faith — in words that reflect his broad experience, understanding of contemporary problems and deep wisdom. 144 pages; Cloth $2.00; Paper $1.00

THE CHURCH — LIGHT OF ALL MANKIND POPE PAUL VI. COMPILED BY THE DAUGHTERS OF ST. PAUL. What is the Church? Who are the People of God? What is the Church's attitude toward the modern world? How does the Church contribute to the advance of social justice? These and many other vital issues are dealt with by Pope Paul VI in this timely book. 156 pages; Cloth $2.00; Paper $1.00

CIVIL RIGHTS – A Source Book. COMPILED BY CHARLES DOLLEN. An introduction to Catholic thinking on the issues involved in the civil rights crusade drawn from official sources: statements of modern Popes, American Bishops, the New Testament, the documents of Vatican II.   162 pages; Cloth $2.00; Paper $1.00

A SUMMONS TO RACIAL JUSTICE BY RICHARD CARDINAL CUSHING. Brief but thorough. His Eminence has penned a vital booklet on a topic of major import. 24 pages; $.06. Special discount of 40% on orders of over 100 copies.

THE CHURCH IN OUR DAY A COLLECTIVE PASTORAL LETTER BY THE BISHOPS OF THE UNITED STATES. A doctrinal exposition of the life and development of the American Catholic Church in the light of Vatican II. 104 pages; Paper 60c; Pamphlet form 35c. *Special rates on bulk orders.*

THE CHRISTIAN AND THE COMMUNITY "Faces up with generous and courageous heart to one's duties as a member of a family, of a civic and national community, as a citizen of the world." WORSHIP.
32 pages; 15c

MORAL VALUES AND THE AMERICAN SOCIETY A vigorous document to foster spiritual life and to restore to the public order those lasting values which undergird our Christian culture. FROM THE INTRODUCTION.   48 pages; 25c

FUNDAMENTALS OF CHRISTIAN SOCIOLOGY BY VERY REV. JAMES ALBERIONE, S.S.P., S.T.D. "...a primer in Christian sociology ...didactic chapters on man and society, the family, civil society, etc., basic questions are asked, blunt answers returned, papal documents cited from Leo XIII to John XXIII. "A good book for discussion clubs." TODAY'S FAMILY   188 pages; Cloth $2.50 Paper $1.50

THE CHURCH AND THE CHANGE BY REV. ROBERT H. HOWES. "Father Howes writes with unusual insight into the contemporary problems of urban renewal, suburbia, planning and metropolitan organization" CATHOLIC MANAGEMENT JOURNAL 316 pages; Cloth $3.50; Paper $2.50

QUESTIONS AND ANSWERS ON COMMUNISM BOOKLET II BY HIS EMINENCE, RICHARD CARDINAL CUSHING. This is a valuable booklet for classes and study groups. "A book of patent questions and definitive answers; most informative and interesting." J. EDGAR HOOVER, DIRECTOR F.B.I. 248 pages; $1.25; Available in French and Spanish $1.00   *50% discount on 50 copies or more.*

THE LAWYER IN COMMUNISM – MEMOIRS OF A LAWYER BEHIND THE IRON CURTAIN *Dr. Lajos Kálmán.* Valuable as an indictment of Communist tyranny. 196 pages; Cloth $3.00; Paper $2.00

WORLD COMMUNISM IN REVIEW BY HENRY R. HUTTENBACK. A current summary of some aspects of Communist dogma, history and tactics.   64 pages 50c

DAUGHTERS OF ST. PAUL

In Massachusetts
  50 St. Paul's Avenue
    Boston, Mass. 02130
  172 Tremont Street
    Boston, Mass. 02111
  381 Dorchester Street
    So. Boston, Mass. 02127
  325 Main Street
    Fitchburg, Mass. 01420

In New York
  78 Fort Place
    Staten Island, N.Y. 10301
  625 East 187th Street
    Bronx, N.Y. 10458
  525 Main Street
    Buffalo, N.Y. 14203

In Connecticut
  202 Fairfield Avenue
    Bridgeport, Conn. 06603

In Ohio
  141 West Rayen Avenue
    Youngstown, Ohio 44503
  415 Euclid Avenue
    Cleveland, Ohio 44114

In Florida
  2700 Biscayne Blvd.
    Miami, Florida 33137

In Louisiana
  86 Bolton Avenue
    Alexandria, La. 71301

In Texas
  114 East Main Plaza
    San Antonio, Texas 78205

In California
  1570 Fifth Avenue
    San Diego, Calif. 92101
  278 - 17th Street
    Oakland, Calif. 94612

In Canada
  8885 Blvd. Lacordaire
  St. Leonard Deport-Maurice
    Montreal, Canada
  1063 St. Clair Avenue West
    Toronto, Canada

In Australia
  58 Abbotsford Road
    Homebush N.S.W., Australia

In Africa
  Box 4392
    Kampala, Uganda

In England
  29 Beauchamp Place
    London, S.W. 3, England

In India
  Water Field Road Extension
  Plot N. 143
    Bandra, India

In Philippine Islands
  No. 326 Lipa City
    Philippine Islands